WHAT I WOULD HAVE MISSED

Stories by Suicide
Ideation, Attempt, and Loss
Survivors

JULIE A ROCCO

What I Would Have Missed
Imprint JAR of Fireflies Productions

Published by What I Would Have Missed; Imprint JAR of Fireflies Productions
Florida, United States
Library of Congress Control Number: 2026907362
ISBN Hardcover: 979-8-9953188-0-4
ISBN Paperback: 979-8-9953188-2-8
ISBN E-Pub: 979-8-9953188-1-1

First Edition
Book Design by Chandler Kennedy
This book contains personal narratives related to suicide ideation, suicide attempts, and suicide loss. It is offered as lived experience and reflection. It is not a substitute for professional medical, psychological, or crisis support.
If you are experiencing thoughts of self-harm or are in immediate distress, please contact emergency services in your area or a suicide prevention hotline. In the United States, you may call or text 988 to reach the Suicide & Crisis Lifeline.
Printed in the United States of America

DEDICATION

*This book is dedicated to Josie, my sister, whose love beckoned our Pop
to make the two-hour drive south because she was 24 hours away.*

*This book is dedicated to my Pop,
who drove the two hours, found me after my attempt and saved my life,
and whose presence, even after his death, continues to shape my
understanding of love, loss, grief, and the slow work of healing.*

*This book is dedicated to my mom and Merrill, my stepdad, who
opened their home to me for months, a home that became a refuge for
my grief and a wellspring of possibility for a future I could begin to
imagine again.*

*This book is dedicated to Zach and Nick, my sons,
and to family and friends
who stood with me in the aftermath of loss
and in the uncertainty of my journey
and the search for a reason I deserve to stay.*

*This book is dedicated to Jeff, my big brother, who consistently walks
beside me through life's valleys with love and compassion, reminding me I
will reach the other side.*

*And it is dedicated to the life I live now that is
shaped by loss and survival, grief and grace, hardship and healing,
which asks me to stay for the moments I do not want to miss.*

*This book is dedicated to anyone touched by suicide.
May you find connection, companionship, and comfort here.*

EMOTIONAL PRINCIPLES

This book was created with care for the many ways people come to these pages.

You may read slowly or quickly. You may pause, skip ahead, or close the book and return another time. There is no single way to move through what is written here.

Some pages may feel familiar. Others may feel distant, difficult, or unexpectedly tender. You are not required to resolve, understand, or respond to everything you encounter here.

Notice what feels grounding. Step away from what feels too heavy. Listening to yourself is part of the work of care.

The stories and reflections in this book are offered as lived experience, not instruction. They are shared to reduce isolation, not to prescribe meaning or outcome.

This book is not a substitute for professional support, crisis care, or community connection. It may, however, sit alongside those supports as a companion when you choose.

This book, at its core, recognizes the power of sharing one's story as both a place of healing for the storyteller and a source of hope for the reader. It honors yours and that of those whose experiences are shared here.

Take what serves you. Leave the rest. Love yourself fiercely.

ABOUT THE STORIES IN THIS BOOK

The stories shared in this book are lived experience, offered exactly as they were submitted.

They have not been rewritten, edited for clarity, grammatically corrected, or adjusted to align with academic, clinical, or professional language. They may use words or phrasing that some would choose to reshape, soften, or censor. They may be nonlinear, imperfect, or unresolved.

That is intentional.

These stories are included in their original form to honor the authentic voices of those who shared them. They reflect how people make meaning in their own words whether raw, real, hopeful, healing, heartbreaking, and honest. Each story holds the truth of the person who lived it at the moment they chose to share.

This book does not attempt to interpret, diagnose, correct, or contextualize these experiences through a clinical lens. It is not a clinical text, a treatment guide, or a substitute for professional care. It should not be read or used as such.

Instead, this book offers space for recognition, companion, and connection. It is a place where lived experience can exist without being filtered, hidden, explained, or translated. The stories are shared not to instruct, but to reduce isolation and remind readers that they are not alone in what they carry.

You are invited to meet these stories as they are, and to engage with them in ways that feel safe and respectful to you.

LEGAL NOTICE & DISCLAIMER

This book is provided for informational and reflective purposes only. The author is not acting as a licensed clinician, medical professional, or mental health provider. Nothing in this book constitutes medical, psychological, or therapeutic advice. This book is not intended to diagnose, treat, cure, or prevent any condition and must not be used as a substitute for professional care or crisis support.

The lived experience stories and reflections included in this book represent personal perspectives and are not presented as guidance, recommendations, or best practices. Individual experiences and outcomes vary. Each name appears in the way its author chose to be known.

If you or someone you know is experiencing distress or thoughts of self-harm, seek assistance from a qualified professional or local emergency services. In the United States, you may call or text 988 to reach the Suicide & Crisis Lifeline. International crisis resources are listed elsewhere   in the resources section of this book.

This book is offered in the spirit of compassion, understanding, and connection. Readers are encouraged to engage with its contents in ways that feel safe and appropriate for their individual needs.

TABLE OF CONTENTS

Author's Letter 19

The Small Things That Anchor Me......................................25
    A Note About Grounding, Reflection, & Journaling................49
    Grounding...51
    Journaling & Reflection Practice................................53

The Ones Who Help Me Through 61
    Grounding...83
    Journaling & Reflection Practice................................85

The Love I Found Or That Found Me...................................93
    Grounding..121
    Journaling & Reflection Practice...............................123

The Generations Across Time 131
    Grounding..153
    Journaling & Reflection Practice...............................155

Discovering Meaning and Purpose.....................................163
    Grounding..187
    Journaling & Reflection Practice...............................189

The Bravest Thing I Ever Did..197
    Grounding..227
    Journaling & Reflection Practice...............................229

What Have I Been Doing These Days? Healing 237
    Grounding..263
    Journaling & Reflection Practice...............................265

Statistics And Insights 273
    The Scope 275
    Who Is Impacted 277
    Contributing Factors...279
    Protective Factors...280
    Treatment And Recovery 281
    A Note On Warning Signs..282
    Data And Resources Informed By 283
    Resources If You Or Someone You Know Needs Immediate Support ...284
    Dear One Who Is Still Here 285

Acknowledgements..291
About The Author..293

"One day you will tell your story of how you overcame what you went through and it will be someone else's survival guide."

Brene Brown

AUTHOR'S LETTER
by Julie A Rocco

The day I came home and discovered my partner had died by suicide, time did not simply stand still. It fractured.

There are moments that divide a life into before and after. That afternoon became mine.

I had left for work believing in the ordinary rhythm of the day. When I returned home, that rhythm was gone. What replaced it was not only grief but also rupture. Everything that felt steady dissolved at once. The future, the plans, the quiet assumptions about tomorrow had all collapsed into a silence I did not yet know how to survive.

Grief arrived immediately. But it did not arrive alone.

It brought questions.

Why didn't I answer the phone when called earlier that afternoon?

Why didn't I come home from work sooner?

Why didn't I recognize how much danger my significant other was in?

Why didn't I see what now felt impossible to miss?

The why questions did not fade. They circled. They sharpened. They nested in the quiet spaces of my mind and replayed themselves without mercy. For many suicide loss survivors, grief carries guilt and blame beside it. There is a persistent belief that one different decision might have rewritten the ending.

In the months that followed, my life began to unravel in visible ways. The house slipped into foreclosure. I filed for bankruptcy. I could not hold a job. My credit collapsed. Structures that once held me upright fell away one by one.

But the deeper collapse happened inside me.

Depression does not always arrive as chaos. Sometimes it is narrowing. The world becomes smaller. Conversations blur. Joy feels distant. Even hope begins to look like something meant for other people.

Inside my thoughts, there was a kind of civil war. Some voices pleaded with me to stay. They were the voices of my children, my family, the people who loved me. Others carried accusation and blame. They replayed the why questions. They insisted I had failed in ways that could not be repaired.

The noise grew louder. I was drowning in the reverberations of could've, would've, should've decisions I was unable to rewind and replay in an effort to arrive at a different outcome. Suicide loss remained as the persistent ending.

In that suffering, there came a moment when I did not want to die, but I could no longer imagine how to continue living. That distinction matters. I was not trying to abandon the people who loved me. I was trying to escape pain I did not know how to survive.

The mind can reach a place where endurance feels impossible, anguish seems permanent, and imagination collapses. When pain eclipses imagination, it can convince you there is no future left to enter.

I believed it.

And in that belief, I became both a suicide loss survivor and then a suicide ideation and attempt survivor.

What followed was not clarity, certainty, or conviction to choose to stay. It was interruption.

Earlier in the day, my sister heard something in my voice she did not recognize and called our father out of concern. He drove two hours south without hesitation. He found me. I was taken to the emergency room and stabilized. Therapy began. A support group was attended. For a time, I moved in with family as I began to navigate a new future. Eventually, I relocated to live near my father and began the slow, uneven work of rebuilding my life while suicidal thoughts had not yet fully loosened their grip.

Staying did not arrive as decisive, declarative or couragous. It arrived as structure.

Appointments kept.

The routine of meditation and exercise.

Conversations that were uncomfortable but necessary.

People who refused to let me disappear quietly.

Survival, I learned, is rarely dramatic. It is repetition. It is accountability. It is allowing yourself to be held when despair would rather isolate. It is participating in the mechanics of living even when meaning has not yet returned.

Meaning came later.

Not all at once. Not as fireworks. But as quiet moments that asked for my attention.

A warm towel fresh from the dryer.

The sound of laughter around a dinner table.

A sunrise that felt gentle instead of indifferent.

Celebrating my son Zach's 30th birthday in Mexico.

Discovering that my heart could open again to falling in love.

Holding my father's hand as he took his final breath.

Watching my son Nick become a father.

Holding my granddaughter Dahlia for the first time.

Moments I never would have lived to see.

I began writing them down. At first, it was not a movement or a mission. It was a practice of noticing. A way to mark the evidence that life was still unfolding for me, even alongside grief, even alongside unanswered questions.

But something began to shift.

When I spoke honestly about surviving both loss and ideation and an attempt, people leaned in. Quiet messages arrived. Stories shared in whispers. Admissions that had been carried alone for years. I began to understand how many people were navigating similar terrain without language, without witness, without a place to lay down what they were holding.

What I Would Have Missed did not begin as an idea for a platform. It began as a recognition: silence deepens despair, and connection loosens it.

We are not meant to endure this kind of darkness in isolation.

The space that grew from those conversations became a place where lived experience could exist without correction, edit, or censorship. Where grief and survival could sit beside one another without hierarchy. Where suicidal thoughts could be acknowledged without shame. Where someone could say, "I have stood there too," and be met with understanding rather than alarm.

Connection, even quiet, imperfect connection, can create the smallest opening where possibility begins to return and light may enter.

If you are reading this while carrying your own version of the why questions, I do not assume to know your story.

If you are grieving someone you love, I do not pretend that survival stories erase your loss.

If you are living with thoughts you have never spoken aloud, I do not insist that hope feels accessible right now.

If you are fighting your way to a life you are imagining for yourself, I do not minimize the battlefield of demons you must conquer to take that first step toward that life.

Instead, I offer something steadier.

I have stood at the edge.

I have listened to the noise.

I have believed the distortion.

I have let go.

I have held on.

And I am still here.

There was a time I could not see what might still be waiting for me.

And yet even in that invisibility, it was.

All of it was waiting to unfold.

When I look back now, I do not only see the milestones. I see texture of a life slowly unfolding with friendships, forgiveness, peace returning slowly, the day I could look in the mirror and feel compassion instead of shame.

There was a time I stood at the edge and could not imagine any of it.

If you are here, something in you is still here too. Even if it feels fragile. Even if it feels uncertain.

The stories that follow are lived experience. They are offered gently, without hierarchy, without comparison. They are meant to sit beside each other and you, not instruct you. The journal prompts following the stories offer space, pause, and rest and the opportunity for reflection should you choose.

In my reflections, I have learned life does not always return in grand gestures. It often unfolds quietly; in ways we do not always recognize as healing.

Sometimes it is only the next breath.

Sometimes it is a moment you did not expect to matter.

And sometimes, even in the darkness, you see a glimmer of light and realize you have stayed long enough to witness what you once believed you would never see.

And you whisper, "Wow, this is What I Would Have Missed. I am so glad I stayed."

THE SMALL THINGS THAT ANCHOR ME

"Be faithful in small things because it is in them that your strength lies."

Mother Teresa

Staying is not always anchored in revelation. More often, it is tethered to something small. Not dramatic turning points. Not sudden clarity. Just the quiet, ordinary things that ask for one more day such as a pet waiting to be fed, a child expecting you home, morning light entering the room, the discovery of a new hobby, the release of a new album from your favorite artist, a conversation that invigorates the mind, a warm cup of coffee, a routine that gives shape to the hours.

For some, these small responsibilities became anchors in moments of despair. For others, after loss, these same small responsibilities became the reason to rise when grief made movement feel impossible.

Staying does not always come with certainty. It does not always feel strong or inspiring. Sometimes it feels quiet. Sometimes it feels heavy. Sometimes it is simply the next small act of care that carries a person forward when everything else feels uncertain.

These pages honor the steady courage found in ordinary care. It is the kind that does not draw attention to itself. The kind that unfolds in kitchens, in cars, in workplaces, in early mornings and late nights.

Sometimes staying, or continuing after loss, begins with tending to what is in front of you. Small. Simple. Steady. Stay. Repeat.

And sometimes that is enough to carry you into another day.

My dog needs a bath my lizard wants more crickets and my cat
was begging for a brush today
My boss said I was his most important employee
My sister called me
I seen a house sparrow with red feathers

Cole H

Someone is smiling today bc of something kind you said to them in passing. "oh I like your earrings" stuck with that person as they are putting them on this morning. The lady you told had on a very pretty blouse was going through more than she thought she could handle and you made her day simply by telling her what a nice blouse she had on. Be kind people. You never know what someone else is going through.

Vanessa

I would have missed:
-knowing what true love is like
-becoming a mom (and becoming one for the second time!)
-the smell and taste of coffee
-writing my own poetry

Jasmine L.M.

I wouldn't be a mother.

I wouldn't have ever heard Hayley Williams solo albums.

I wouldn't have heard Billie Eilish.

I wouldn't have watched cw's the Flash

I would have never discovered my favorite taco bus.

Never gotten any sick ass tattoos

Never discovered my love for being an oddeties artist

I would have never learned to drive a car

I wouldn't know what it's like to live in a house that we own!

I wouldn't know my sweet dog

Never would have met my 3 best friends

Never would have been truly in love

Tiffanie

If I had been successful? I would have missed my family adopting my cousin to be my sister, she's my best friend now. I would've never graduated or even made it through high school. I would've never gotten into my dream college. I would've never gotten my tortoise, whom I adore with all my heart. I would've never gotten back in touch with my girlier side. I would've never stopped labeling myself. I would've never even seen my baby sister into middle school...I would've missed a lot.

Victoria

I would've missed finding the love of my life—the kindest man I've ever met. I would've missed adopting a dog. I would've missed my new bands next 3 albums—all of which brought me great joy. I would've never gotten past the part of life where I felt I was inherently broken and I definitely never would've experienced genuine peace or happiness or being proud of myself. But I didn't do it, so I did.

Dawson

When I started to see my potential small at first but when I stopped to look I also saw possibilities…I knew then I could live with myself…and love what I could become.

Sheldon

Love. So much love was waiting for me, but I wasn't ready yet. I'm glad I decided to stay and change what I could about the life I wanted to escape. Things got so much better after some time, effort, and luck I never imagined. The tiniest change helped in the big picture, and I couldn't have happened if I wasn't here.

Hina

I have suffered from depression most of my life and several times I've strongly felt I didn't want to be here anymore and acted on it. I still sometimes think I don't want to be here anymore but I no longer act on it. Almost 13 years ago I got a call I wish no one would ever get. A good friend, a man I loved, the father of my twins, make the final choice. Our children have no memory of him and I have to believe that if he had known how much he would miss and how many people would miss him, he would've made a different choice. Our kids have grown up so amazingly and I hate that he hasn't been there for any of it.

I know a lot of times it can feel like no one cares, that things just aren't worth the pain, some days are really hard, but people do care, even people that don't know you, care. You can't know the wonderful things life can bring if you're not here for it.

M

My father recently made the decision to end his life and though it has been devastating, I am trying to look through the lens of love. Today I choose to honor him and his memory, by staying. Staying and living double (for the both of us). See, life can get really, really heavy sometimes…and I have been in that dark, desperate place myself. So I can understand how he (or others like my father) feel/felt. I never wish that upon anyone. So I choose to live my life in a way that shows love and compassion for all. I can't "fix" others but I CAN do my part in helping them to feel loved, genuinely listened to, and appreciated… By all accounts, it is a miracle that I am even here today but I'm so glad I am. To behold a sunrise, a child's laughter, a romantic kiss, a four-leaf clover, precious moments spent with family.. Makes the harder days worth fighting through. Life is so fragile but it is worth every single second. Stay' Your story isn't over. YOU MATTER.

Brittany

I would've missed my two hound dogs.

I would've missed the sky and the sounds of birds, and feeling the sun on my skin. I would've missed the feeling of running through the hot sand on a beach and diving into the ocean, and listening to the sounds of kids and seagulls in the distance.

I would've missed my Mom. The way she starts a phone call, and the way her house smells. The way she still reads the newspaper on her porch in the morning, and I would've missed our fights.

I would've missed laughing with my friends until my stomach hurt. I would've missed listening to the music loud while driving with the windows down at night. I would've missed the smell of my dog's paw, drinking Baja Blast, and skateboarding. I would've missed painting and writing and working with kids & telling people they're important.

I would've missed the subtle comfort of the light on above the stove at night, and the complete joy being sandwiched between my two dogs in bed.

I would've missed making plans and dreaming about big things for my life. I would've missed holding my best friend's baby for the first time, and seeing the people I love—happy. I would've missed crying and feeling things deeply.

I would've missed figuring out my place here.

For all the pain and heartbreak…for the countless times I've tried to convince myself it isn't worth staying—I am really glad I don't have to miss it.

Arden

Three years ago, my life split in two when my sister, Jade, passed by suicide. There is a version of me that existed before that day, and a version of me that was born from it. In the beginning, I was consumed by questions with no answers. I replayed conversations, searched for signs, and carried guilt that was never mine to hold. Suicide grief is not just sadness. It is shock in the nervous system, love with nowhere to land, anger and compassion in the same breath. The day I found out she passed, a dragonfly landed on my thigh and stayed. I didn't understand it then, but it has come to symbolize transformation. How something can break you open and still become light. I have learned this: Jade was not defined by how she passed. She was depth, sensitivity, laughter, and a heart that felt everything. And she mattered.

Losing her forced me to confront the silence around suicide. The stigma, the discomfort, the things left unsaid. I had to unlearn the belief that talking about it would make it worse. Silence almost cost us everything. I refuse to let it have the final word. Grief has reshaped me, but it has also strengthened me. It has taught me to sit with pain and to tell the truth, even when my voice shakes. I carry Jade with me in how I love, listen, and show up. Her life continues through the compassion I give to others. That is how I honor her.

If you are grieving someone lost to suicide, or quietly wondering if staying is worth it, I am speaking to you. I live inside the ripple suicide leaves behind. I know the devastation and the ache that doesn't have words. To the grieving heart: your feelings can coexist. There is no right way to carry this. To the struggling heart: your pain deserves support, not silence. Your life matters in ways you cannot see. Staying is brave. Reaching out is strength. If sharing Jade's story helps even one person feel less alone, then her life continues to create connection, courage, and hope.

Kaitlyn Armstrong
June 2022
In loving memory of Jade

What did she miss

Her baby growing into a beautiful little person

Sunny days during winter with me here in Florida—unlimited pork chops..lol..midnight margartitas.

Reunions with her brothers on a beach..unlimited laughter and sunshine

Struggle food that we both loved..brunches by the sea..dancing with her gimpy mom under a full moon or at dusk when the sunset is perfect

My double vanity covered with every form of makeup and lotions you can think of

Bike rides all over town to buy plants and flowers

Nell V

When you disappeared from the earth a little over two years ago, you missed out on your little niece being born. Her name is Abigail; We love you. I'll always miss you, and she hears about you all the time.

Hanna
RIP: 9/29/2023
In loving memory of Christopher

I lost my big sister to suicide 9/7/24. Just had her one year memory.
I miss her so much. When I meditate I swear I can hear her wisdom.

Ashley

Getting engaged. Moving into our home. My sister graduating and becoming a beautiful woman. I'd miss my pawpa a lot. And my best friends babies. And my mom and my dad. And my brother and sister. And my partner. We're all here for a reason. Rather that reason be big or small, you're here for a reason. You're going to make an impact on someone's life even if you don't remember it. Strangers will look at you and think you're beautiful and you won't even know but that's just the little impact that someone can make on someone else. You are here. Not by mistake. For a reason. You mean something. Someone love you. You are one of a kind. God made YOU by hand for a reason.

Zoe W

Pause.

Take a slow breath.

Let your body settle.

A NOTE ABOUT GROUNDING, REFLECTION & JOURNALING

As you move through these pages, you may be reminded of your own experiences. Thoughts, feelings, and memories may surface, some easily, others slowly.

Throughout the book, you will encounter moments set aside for reflection through journaling or quiet pause. These pages are woven intentionally between lived experience stories to offer space to process and turn inward.

These invitations are not assignments. They are spaces.

You might choose to write. You might sit quietly and let a thought unfold without capturing it. You may draw. One word may offer full expression. You may return to a page later, or turn past one entirely.

Reflection does not require performance. It simply offers a place for honesty to land in whatever form it arrives.

Sometimes putting words or images on paper creates room where there once felt like none. Sometimes naming a feeling softens its edges. Sometimes nothing comes at all and that, too, is part of your experience.

These pages are here as companions and quiet spaces alongside the stories. How you use them is entirely your own.

If at any point the reflections feel overwhelming, pause. Place your feet on the floor. Take a slow breath in and a longer breath out. Remind yourself that you are here, in this moment. And, that is enough.

GROUNDING PRACTICE

Press your feet firmly into the floor.
Name five things you see.
Take one slow breath in and a longer breath out.
You are here.
That is enough for this moment.

JOURNALING & REFLECTION PRACTICE

Take a moment to turn inward.
Let these questions meet you where you are.

Small things steady us. Loss changes the shape of the small things that once steadied us.

When you are ready, start with something small that helps you stay.

1. What small, ordinary things in your life quietly anchor you, even if they do not feel significant?

2. How do these small things help you remain for another day, and which one might you choose to hold onto tomorrow?

Carry forward what feels grounding, comforting and supportive.
Allow everything else to rest and remain here.

THE ONES WHO HELP ME THROUGH

"So, from all of us at Aerosmith, to all of you out there wherever you are, remember, the light at the end of the tunnel may be you. Goodnight."

Aerosmith, from the song Amazing

Support shapes many of the stories that follow highlighting the people who help someone move through hard hours and heavy seasons. Not always with perfect words. Not always with answers. But with presence.

Support can look like intervention in a moment of crisis. It can look like someone refusing to let you disappear quietly. It can also be the steady companionship that follows suicide loss such as the friend who stays when grief changes you, the family member who helps carry practical burdens when everything feels altered, the therapist who listens without rushing resolution or attempting to explain what cannot be explained.

Help can arrive in many forms. A friend who listens. A teacher who notices. A coach who encourages. A therapist who steadies. A neighbor who checks in. A colleague who offers grace. After loss, it may be the person who sits in silence beside you, who remembers the name of the one you love, who allows their absence to remain present.

Support does not erase struggle. It does not undo what has happened. It does not restore what has been lost. But it can soften isolation. It can remind someone that their life touches other lives and that even in grief, connection remains possible.

Connection does not solve everything, but it can steady the ground beneath you.

Sometimes it is enough to know you are not alone.

The birth of my nephews and nieces. Winning a lacrosse championship, meeting Curtis Joseph, meeting my friends, meeting my best friend, my dogs.

Stephanie

I would've missed gaining a sister and having 2 hilarious and adorable nephews. I would've missed seeing the day where my family actually got a cat. I would've missed so many late nights with some of my favorite people dancing around laughing and sharing memories. I would've missed finding people who didn't make me feel like I was crazy and a burden and instead made me feel loved cared for and needed. I would've missed mine and my brother's graduation. I would've missed so much incredible music that I now can't go a single day without. I would've missed that one although undoubtedly inappropriate but still absolutely funny and unforgettable comment grandpa made and that one day where grandma and me talked all day about everything from basic recipes to deep family secrets that now lay with only us. I would've missed finding my passion in cooking art and writing. I would've missed being able to see the day where I have a family a real genuine family even though none of them are my blood they mean the absolute world to me and they help me get though the hardest of days and don't even know it.

Charlotte

I would have missed this loving relationship who cares a lot about me. He even helped me through alcohol rehab. I didn't think I'd live past 25. We're together and I'm almost 33.

H.L.W.

Everything got me down and I could see no way out so I made plans to kill myself. I was about to go through with it when my best friend came threw my door and shouted at me, what the hell are you doing. This is not the answer. He talked to me and saved my life, only for that I was gone. I got help as soon as I could and I told people on Facebook what I was going through and the amount of people that cared about me was unreal. I would have missed Armagh winning the all Ireland football. I would have missed my best friends who cared.

Neely / Northern Ireland

I attempted in 2010…was in a coma for 6 months. Every time I see the beauty in the sky, in my husband's face, the people that love me. My best friend. I see exactly what I would be missing and I stay away from the edge the best I can. Theyre all worth it to not YOLO my life like that again.

Katrina M

I would have missed a lot of the best things to have happened in my life. I wouldn't have seen my brother defy all odds and graduate high school. I wouldn't have met some of the most kind, caring and compassionate people who are part of the reason I keep going every single day. I wouldn't have met my significant other only 5 years later and started the family we have today. I wouldn't have seen the moon another 3, 360 days and counting. I wouldn't have found an amazing therapist who helps me learn to heal, grow, and find new reasons to be grateful and happy to be here today. I would have missed the opportunity to write this message. The sadness, pain, anger, whatever it is you're feeling/going through doesn't last forever. It gets better.

Emily

If I had succeeded, in my 25th summer, I never would have gotten married to the love of my life. The same person who saved it that day. I never would have grown from the crisis point I was in towards the person I wanted to be. I would've missed out on my life's purpose, on amazing lives and passings that taught me so much. After I survived, I finally started to live. Really live.

Mako

I have struggled with my mental health my entire life and did not get a diagnosis until last year. Growing up undiagnosed doesn't mean symptom-free, it means feeling alone in your symptoms. And my scariest one, among panic attacks, exhaustion episodes, crying spells and rejection sensitivity, has been suicidal ideation. There were so many difficult moments where it seemed like the only option, one of them being the summer I was fifteen. I had struggled with my issues for so long, I felt defeated, rejected, and done. I stood in my room thinking about a way I could end it all in under a half hour and staring at a clock. God protected me; I survived that and many moments after it. Since then, so many amazing things have happened. A girl I knew at the time but not well became my best friend, the closest friend I've ever had who knows my struggles, has gone through things with me, and truly loves me and sees me for who I am. I experienced a very traumatic breakup that showed me who my real friends are. I found some of my favorite music artists! God brought me so much closer to Him through worship, prayer, the Bible and my amazing church. I got my driver's license and my quirky car. I can—sometimes even easily—resist the desire to self-harm now. I got on medication that has been so helpful. I got my diagnosis, not a "label" but an explanation and a pathway to healing. I have done college classes and am going to do my dream job someday. In fact, I found a current job where I have developed real resilience, practical skills and amazing friendships. Even though I still have bad days, I look forward to working, to school, to seeing my best friend, to cuddling up to spend some time in prayer and Bible reading. It's worth it, even if it feels like it isn't sometime. Don't let the hard days win, and listen, if you are reading this, you ARE winning. As longs as you are alive, you are winning.

Amelia

What I would have missed….has brought me back from the edge of my darkness many times.

I'm a suicide survivor, as well as, a soul touched too many times by friends and loved ones that couldn't see what they would miss.

I've struggled with depression and the desire to go home as far back as I can remember. I tried when I was 11 and 13. My dad got me help, but then he got Cancer and the darkness swallowed my light.

My last attempt I was in my late 20s. I had 2 sons and 2 divorces. I was a failure. I never could do anything right. I was lost. My cognitive thinking was way out of kilter. I fell in the bottle.

I was working for the Highway Patrol, Chief Investigator, at the time and my Chief sent me to Employee Assistance because he saw my pain. They sent me to be assessed, and she decided I needed to be admitted for observation. Wait. My sons are waiting for me to pick them up.

Who will pick them up if you're gone?

That flipped my switch, if I'm gone I won't see my sons play sports, or band, or anything. I would have missed my best friend my daughter. I would have missed my 2 grandsons, 3 granddaughters. I would have missed my son coming back from the war zone.

The very things that broke my heart because Dad was missing them saved my life. I've told my sons they saved my life. I've promised if ever the darkness starts to close in I will call.

I am now doing all that I can to reach out to others, especially veterans, to bring more awareness, to honor and remember those who lost their wars and help their loved ones in any way I can.

Gini S

In Junior High & High School, I went through major depression due to bullying. I had a plan, & I had access, but a teacher who knew I was considering quitting choir told me "if you quit, they win. " That statement saved my life over & over through the years. Eventually, High school ended & instead of bullies, "they" turned into hard days. If I quit, the hard days win. I am the type to over-analyse most of my decisions. In this case, it helped save my life, because I think about what the action would solve: the problem would still be there, but I wouldn't. That means I would have lost & left the pieces for someone else to pick up. I didn't want to pass on the pain that others caused me, so I hung onto scripture. Hebrews 13: 5-6 became my life verse, telling me that I'm not alone & that I have a helper. One of the musicals we did in high school, I.M.A.G.E., also taught me that I have a purpose, because I am Made in God's image. Accepted as His in spite of who I am or what I've done. Given new life through His sacrifice. Eternally united with Him. I looked back on this over the years & reminded myself that as long as God kept me alive on this earth, it meant He wasn't done with me. I still had a purpose. I have value, because He decided I was worth dying for. I am not alone, because I am Eternally united with Him & He walks through this life with me. As long as I hold onto these truths, I know that difficulties I go through will not destroy me. I am not going through it alone & difficult times will not last forever.

Since high school & college, I have gotten married, seen friends' weddings, & become a mother. I would have missed all of that if I had died back then. In 2025, I lost my brother to suicide. Before that, I didn't even know he had been struggling. Depression & anxiety returned as part of the grief, but I am not interested in harming myself. I have a front row seat seeing what that does to the family. Instead, I am researching how to help others not have to go through this. Helping others is helping me.

Christine Melson

Most people never understand this constant battle that those of us with depression face every minute of our lives! I would have missed my oldest son being ordained as a minister. He and his wife finally being blessed with our first granddaughter. I would have missed my daughter graduating high school, college and getting her masters. I would have missed out on taking in her best friend and giving her a better life. Allowing her to see what marriage is about and that someone believed in her. Watching her graduate high school and go on to graduate college. Watching my oldest son play football. Watching my girls do color guard and winter guard. I would have missed my youngest son excel at sports, be everyone's friend and be loved by everyone he knows! I would have not been here to keep him alive more times than I can count over a 3 year period as his addiction overtook him. I would not have been here to celebrate his 1st year of sobriety. I would have missed out on all the love my husband has to give. I would have missed out on being able to help care for my Dad when he was sick. I wouldn't have been here for my husband and children when my father in law passed away due to COVID. I wouldn't have been here to take care of my Grandmother after my Dad passed until the very minute Alzheimer's robbed her of her last breath.

My story is too long to go into...but I wouldn't have been in the class at the mental health facility when they told me about how depression and suicide effects the children. That hit hard! I also wouldn't have been there for the phone call where my daughter told me she had sought out therapy. She was in the early part of freshman year at college. She started having anxiety and some panic attacks and that if it had not been for seeing what I was going through she wouldn't have known to seek help! She is now a mental health therapist and social worker. I would have missed out on being her muse and my best friend!

Brandy

My brother took his own life at the young age of 31. He was a single father of two children. Their mother was never around, so the weight of being a single parent, bills, and life in general just got the best of him. His daughter is in the national honor society, with a GPA of 3.5+. His son, following in his footsteps and playing the guitar. My husband and I adopted them both after. His passing, while raising 6 of our own. We now have a very large family, but that's okay. We ordered her senior ring last night, and I couldn't help but wish he was here being the one doing this with her. His son is learning some Metallica on his dad's very first guitar that we restored and he is doing so wonderful. My brother would be proud. His daughter is driving now, and her brother isn't far behind her. Christmas is coming, but the holidays aren't the same anymore. He should be here with us. He should be doing all of these things with us and preparing his daughter for college. He should be wiping the tears from her eyes over silly boys instead of my wiping them from him leaving us. He should be beside his son teaching him all he knows on the guitar and beating us all at guitar hero. But, he isn't. And that is something that will forever ache my heart. I wish we could go. Back and change things. Talk things through. Realize that life does go on. And things do get better. The hard times are only a phase of life that we learn from and then we move forward. Keep going, keep pushing even when you feel like you can't anymore. You may be surprised at how different life could be.

Sidney
RIP: 05/27/22
In loving memory of Jordan

Lost my son at 17 on 7/27/2025. I will miss his graduation high school and college, his marriage, his children, and most of all his voice and hugs.

Jean MG

First of all it would be my heart and world. My daughter. There's so much that I would've missed but I'll try to condense it down. The love that I have been slowly getting over the last 5 years from those who aren't blood related but those who decided to stay in my corner and love me for me. The laughs and sore sides I would get from laughing with my friends (whom I wouldn't have known either had I been successful) when we would be major dorks together without caring about looking weird. The beautiful sites I see within the skies and lands.

Gorgeous scenery paintings that God makes while we all go about our daily lives. There's so much more and there will always be more to add and I can't wait to add more and to get to know more souls are just like me and just trying to make it another day. Wanting to feel loved. If no one has said it to you today…I love you. I'm glad you're here with me in this moment in time. May you have a beautiful and bright future.

Heather C

Pause.

Take a slow breath.

Let your body settle.

GROUNDING PRACTICE

Place one hand on your chest.

Place the other on something solid such as a chair, a table, your leg.

Feel your body supported.

Breathe in slowly.

Breathe out slowly.

You do not have to solve anything right now.

You do not have to decide anything right now.

For this moment, simply notice that you are breathing.

That is enough.

JOURNALING & REFLECTION PRACTICE

Take a moment to turn inward.
Let these questions meet you where you are.

Support may come through a teacher, therapist, friend, family member, coach, or trained listener. It may come through someone who intervened in a moment of crisis, or someone who simply stayed when the silence felt heavy. For loss survivors, support may look like the person who speaks the name of the one you love, who sits beside your grief without trying to solve it.

When you are ready, reflect on the forms of support that have held you in crisis, in grief, or in the long stretch between.

1. Who has helped you through difficult seasons?

2. If reaching out feels possible, is there someone you may consider contacting this week? If so, how might you begin? If not, what support might you wish were easier to ask for?

Carry forward what feels grounding, comforting and supportive.
Allow everything else to rest and remain here.

THE LOVE I FOUND

OR THAT FOUND ME

"The wound is the place where the light enters you."

Rumi

What shapes us most deeply is often connection. It is the kind that opens the heart and asks us to be known. Not perfect love. Not love without difficulty. But love that meets us in our humanity.

Love can take many forms. It may be romantic. It may be chosen family. It may be a friendship that grows into something enduring. It may be the quiet realization that someone sees you clearly and stays anyway. It may be the love that remains after someone is gone. The love that grief will never erase.

Love does not erase wounds. It does not undo the past. But it can bring light into places that once felt closed off. It can remind us that we are worthy of care, of tenderness, of being understood even when we carry wounds and scars.

These stories are shared as glimpses of what may unfold, of what is possible, of what can grow even in seasons when it feels distant or hard to imagine. They are reminders that connection can arrive in unexpected ways and at unexpected times.

Connection does not solve everything and it does not remove loss. But it can open space inside us that pain once filled and where life continues alongside it.

And sometimes that opening is enough to begin again.

I had picked a day, i picked a time when no one would be home. It was quiet and the house was still. I was going to do it in a way so my mom wouldn't have much to clean and there would be little mess. I was molested at a young age, when my mom found out she didnt know how to even go about the situation. I didnt tell her all that happened, it was two of my older cousins and i was raped. I couldnt keep living with the memories, the nightmares, the anxiety and depression. I thought id finally lost and it was time. But as i was preparing myself to die, my boyfriend texted me. He had just got home from school, he said he missed me and he loved me so so much. He had sent me this massive message with so much care and love. I broke down, I thought over so much…so much id miss, so much love i had left to give. I had been so consumed by pain and depression that i had this tunnel vision where i couldnt see how many people id hurt. So many others who may also try what i did without me. I decided to get up, burned the paper with my final message and called my boyfriend. Hes my husband now, i finally told him how he save me. Had I done it that day, i wouldve missed my siblings graduations. I wouldve not been there for them through the hardest phase of my dads abuse. I wouldnt have gotten to see my family get better. I wouldve not been there for my husband through his dad and grandpa dying. We forget that we are a lot of peoples support systems and i forgot that in the worst moment of my life. I hadnt realized that people needed me or wanted me in their lives so much that they would have lost it if they lost me. Im worth something, and so are you. Life goes on, but life needs you to go on. Suicide is the wrong answer to a hard problem. Im glad that i am here. Because i am needed.

Raven

If I would have died during my suicide attempt, I would have missed having my daughter, marrying a man who ACTUALLY loves me and is my best friend. I would of missed walking out of the world of grey I was in and seeing colors again. I would have missed finding myself and not being terrified of my dark side. I can't promise life will always be great but it will be worth it.

Rebecca

I fell head over heels for my Jay right before the pandemic began. Just over a year later, he was gone. I dropped into a hole of addiction, self destructive behaviors, and I was ready to go. I had my death day picked out, the day after my 25th birthday. I thought a friend who had died at 18 would have wanted me to hit 25 and so I held on that long. I was lucky that my therapist intervened and had me hospitalized, gave me enough time to reconsider. I was still absolutely ready to leave this earth, but then, as if by magic, my Dalton dropped into my life. He took the broken parts of me and helped me get them in order enough to keep going and then gave me reasons aplenty to want to stay. Now I'm engaged to my second husband, carrying Jay with me everyday, and I never ever considered I could be this happy.

Benji Lee

My beautiful son each day i think what you could be doing today a life cut short with so many more days weeks months and years to live you have missed your beautiful son grow into an incredible 17 year old man you would be so proud of what he has achieved but most of all you have missed the love we have for you. love mum xx

Sarah
RIP: 13/8/22
In loving memory of George

I would have missed meeting, knowing, and loving, my four youngest nieces and nephews. I would have missed my youngest sister's wedding, seeing all my nieces and nephews grow up and getting to help raise 5 of them. I would have missed their high school graduations, the sleepovers and tea parties, the hugs and kisses, the laughter, the mutual support and friendship I now enjoy with them as young adults. I would have missed witnessing the conversion and beautiful transformation of one of the kids I used to babysit and having the joy and privilege of being part of his wedding this year. I would have missed the chance to see the difference I actually made in another person's life and the continued opportunities I have to offer the same love and hope to others that so many have shown to me. I would have missed the chance to thank the women in my life who loved me even in my mess, and the chance to love and care for my grandma during the last year of her life. What a blessing that was!!!!! I would have missed the chance to apologize to the people in my life that I hurt and make it up to them. And I would have missed the chance to share with all of you how beautiful life is and can be, even through the trials, and encourage you not to give up, because trials are temporary and there's always someone willing and able to help, you just have to ask. So keep asking until you get a yes and know that life IS worth living.

Rachel

It is so funny that this has popped up on my feed as I have been thinking about all the good things I would have missed if I had been successful at ending my life. So, I feel it is fate and just have to do this!

In 2021 I met the most amazing man and we got married in 2025—neither I thought would ever happen. It was so wonderful seeing all our loved ones in one room, there because of our love. My husbands family have become a second family to me which I've never had before and is so lovely. In 2025 I also got to celebrate my Nan's 100th Birthday with her and all the people who adore her, which was her wish. IN 2024 I met a colleague who has now become a wonderful friend. We went to my first Pride in Bristol together in 2025 which was amazing! I FINALLY got my first tattoo in 2025 (I originally was going to get one 8 years prior after attempting suicide) and I love it – and it is definitely not my last! At the end of 2025 I was told I'm going to be a great uncle, not only once, but twice (both my nieces are having a baby)! I am learning to drive (in secret to surprise everyone which will be a shock to them all), which I never thought I would ever do, so I am so proud of myself. I have grown so much and have got to experience so many new things and places that I would have missed out on had I not been here   concerts, food, holidays, weddings, birthdays, seeing loved ones achieve their goals and be by their side whilst they overcome their own battles, and much more. It has been a tough journey to get here and I still have incredibly difficult days and weeks even, but there are so many wonderful moments that I just think "I am so glad I made it here to experience this". Not all of them are even huge moments, sometimes it's just in the most ordinary moments that I realise how lucky I am. Lucky to be here and to have all I have. I have a job I love, a lovely home, wonderful friends, the most supportive husband who I love more than I could ever imagine I could love someone – and he loves me like I've never experienced before. I am truly blessed. And now I am so excited to see what else I would have missed!

Danial H-M from UK

He missed the birth of his son, he missed him growing up into an amazing man. His son misses a man he never knew.

Beth L

My name is Hanna and I'm 24 years old. About five years ago, if you would've asked me, "How old do you think you'll live to be?" my reply would've been, "probably around 21. I can't see myself living longer than that." My first and only true suicide attempt was when I was about 15 years old. I was struggling with drug addiction and mental health issues that made it hard to even wake up in the morning and live my life. Every day was intense suffering. No matter who I hung out with, and no matter what hobbies I did to try to make myself happy, nothing worked. I remember when my ex-boyfriend walked into the room and saw my body. I had just started losing consciousness. Everybody says when you die, you go to heaven; but everything was black. I could hear him crying. He grabbed me and just held me. After that, it was like it never happened. Nobody talked about it, and if someone did bring it up, they didn't take it seriously. Now, being a little over five years sober, I just gave birth to a beautiful little girl. I met the man who I want to spend the rest of my life with, and he's an amazing father to our child. And I have to say, every single bit of pain and suffering seems to have been worth it. I would do anything to see her smile at me and hear her laugh; I'm so happy I stayed alive for her.

Hanna Starche

I was going to share a photo of what I would have missed but I scrolled my camera roll and the answer is I would have missed all of it. I would have missed every picture on that roll. Every person I have met and loved every adventure I've been on. I would have missed it all. I would have never met some of my best friends. I would never have been overseas. I would have never met the love of my life. God, teenage me would never believe how good it got!

Miranda A-D

I would have missed saving my cats. They saved me, but I have saved cats that were abandoned, left on the side of the road or neglected. If I wasn't here, they wouldnt have had a warm bed to share with me, and so many laughs and cuddles. I wouldn't have been here for my friend who felt sad, or my boyfriend who needed love too. I would have missed all these beautiful relationships.

Sarah

Saving the worlds best dog from euthanasia at the shelter, and starting my animal charity.

Kelly

I would have missed learning to love myself and I would have missed seeing my children with trust in their eyes again.

Sara O

I would have missed the personal growth that came after. The part where I now love myself. The light at the end of the tunnel that made staying worth it. I would have missed my son playing school football. I would have missed teaching my daughter how to wash her face or pick out undergarments. I would have missed. My son becoming a teenager and having crushes. I would have missed a long awaited, much needed and wanted reconciliation. I would have missed out on the little things…the laughs, the jokes, the hugs, the "I love you's". I would have missed our new puppy. I would have missed graduations. I would have missed my family. I would not be here but my memory would be here on every special occasion, on every anniversary, on every birthday. I would have left a hole that could never be filled again. I would have missed being me, even on the days I didn't want to be me. Take it one day at a time, one hour at a time, and if you have to, take it one minute at a time. You will be missed so please stay. Please stay for one more day. Make a list of all the things you have to stay for. Add to it. Every little thing matters. Your child's birthday, your child starting middle school, talking to your mom, having a big hug from someone you love, hearing that you are loved. You really matter. You are wanted and you are loved.

Tisha B

I would have missed meeting my moms side after 27 years.

I would have missed starting a business.

I would have missed my four beautiful fur babies.

I would have missed traveling the country.

I would have missed the Pacific Ocean.

I would have missed my dad truly apologizing.

Curvella DB

My 3 nieces and my nephew.

My best friends.

Learning to drive! Getting a car. Sobriety.

Sophie

I would have missed my wedding. It was the best day of my life.

Dakota R

I have had multiple attempts but my most memorable one was at the age of 14 this attempt was incredibly near fatal and I'm lucky to of survived without permanent disability. If I would have succeeded with this attempt I would have missed the many years of struggling after with mental health following this attempt. But i think about this and without those struggles i would not be the person I am today. I struggled for years after the attempt sure, but all of this made me the happy Harlow I am now! I would have missed the guy I have become with my transition, and I would have also missed out on ever meeting my girlfriend. I am an old soul and i love to make peoples days i want nothing more than to be happy and while I always wanted that i previously could rarely achieve it I am 19 now and it's weird because I didn't think id ever live past 13 and than 14 and than 15…and so on, but i am here. And I am one hell of an awesome guy! I love all creatures great and small on rainy days I take walks to the local park and pick up worms on the sidewalk to place them back in the dirt. my laugh is contagious and I love to create art in all forms I mostly work in multimedia works that includes drawing but I also love to work with 3 dimensional pieces. I think if I had succeeded with my attempt i would of missed out on simply living as the person i have grown to be now. I saved this part for last but if I had succeeded with my suicide attempt I would of never met Peeve. Peeve is my rabbit, he was found dumped outside in a rural area in my town. Someone found the clearly domesticated rabbit and posted on the local facebook group. rabbits are often dumped pets and im incredibly knowledgeable on rabbits I knew I had to take him in. rabbits being prey animals have a hard time trusting an often in situations like this they are very scared and can be aggressive. Peeve allowed me to pick him up with ease and take him to the carrier I had in the car. He was very gentle and curious. Peeve warmed up to me incredibly fast and put a lot of trust in me which was beautiful knowing he had already been through so much as just a little rabbit. I haven't even owned Peeve for a year yet but every day I think about how he was just a little miracle from the universe. He was a sign. I've always felt spiritually connected with rabbits and when I changed my name to Harlow many years ago, I felt connected with the name as it literally means "meadow of the hares" Peeve is truly a delight his favorite song is beautiful boy and I used to sing it to him each night but I only do it sometimes now as he had a playlist I play for him that mostly include nirvana and the beatles. Peeve is a die hard Beatles fan. I think about how precious Peeve is to me and how fragile life is. I think about how grateful I am to have Peeve and how I would have missed this had I succeeded 5 years ago.

Harlow

I would've missed realizing that our lives are interconnected with every human, and every living being, and our earth, and our stars, and the source, a.k.a. God, the all knowing and being, that is the present moment.

Now, open your eyes. Close them. Hold them shut. Open them again and what do you see?

Eyes open or closed can see the everlasting and symbiotic relationship that is connected by the space between us.

To see in this sense is to feel.

That little spark of a memory, that little flare of excitement of looking forward to something....

Our memories and our wishes are us, now, and as you read these pages, let them tell you that you are the cloud as much as the rain that fell to the Earth to grow the tree to print the page onto which this is written.

Because it was written for you and me and us.

Beautiful and ugly. All the same. We are one. We are love. And you and I are loved, whether we see it or not.

Scott Callison

I would have missed falling in love with myself and, wow,
she's a catch!

ash

Pause.
Take a slow breath.
Let your body settle.

GROUNDING PRACTICE

Place your hand over your heart.
Notice its rhythm.
Whisper:
"I am still here."
Take three slow breaths.

JOURNALING & REFLECTION PRACTICE

Take a moment to turn inward.
Let these questions meet you where you are.

Some love stays beside us. Some love lives in memory. If anything within these stories touched your own experience of connection or loss, you are invited to pause here, let it unfold gently, and explore what it has meant in your life.

When you are ready, take a moment to reflect on what you carry forward.

1. What forms of love have shaped your life whether still beside you, held in memory, or yet to unfold, that you carry with you?

2. If love feels distant right now, what is one small way you can remain connected to yourself, to memory, or to someone who cares for you?

Carry forward what feels grounding, comforting and supportive.
Allow everything else to rest and remain here.

THE GENERATIONS ACROSS TIME

"We are made of all those who have built and broken us."

Andrea Gibson

Our lives are part of a continuum through time, through memory, through becoming.

We are connected to those who came before us and to those who arrive after. By parents and grandparents. By children and grandchildren. By siblings, cousins, students, friends, chosen family. By the ones who stayed. And by the ones whose absence quietly reshaped the landscape of our lives.

Some generations shape us through presence, through shared meals, long conversations, traditions repeated year after year, advice given in passing, the ordinary rituals that become memory. Others shape us through what was interrupted. Through milestones not witnessed. Through words left unsaid. Through the ache of imagining who they might have continued to become.

For those who have stood at the edge themselves, staying means allowing time to keep unfolding. It means witnessing growth you could not yet see like watching children stretch into their own identities, watching elders soften, noticing your own becoming take shape in ways you once thought impossible. Staying means remaining long enough to see what changes.

For those living with suicide loss, the shaping does not end with death. Love does not end. Influence does not end. Memory becomes part of the continuum. The lives we grieve continue to shape how we live, how we love, how we choose differently. Absence becomes another form of presence, not replacing what was, but reminding us of what mattered.

We are never shaped in isolation. We shape, and we are shaped in return. The way we remain has quiet impact beyond what we can measure. The way others remained, or could not, has shaped who we are now.

The stories in this section reflect that ongoing influence. The way life continues to move. The way becoming does not stop at one moment of despair. The way time, even when marked by grief, keeps unfolding.

Sometimes staying is not only about surviving the present or holding the past. It is about honoring the continuum and allowing yourself to honor the past, be part of the present, and remain for what unfolds next.

If 16 year old me had been successful at ending my life, 40 year old me would never have grown the successful career and beautiful family that I have. I would have missed so many amazing things (a husband, my children, my career, LIFE). At the time I had no idea life could be the way it is now.

Leigh

I would have missed the birth of my daughter who is now my entire reason for living. I also would have missed the impact that I have in the lives of my students and being the adult that I needed growing up.

Roni

What my dad missed since he died by suicide when I was 22. He missed me getting my bachelors and masters degrees. He missed my wedding, he missed the birth and 12yrs so far of his granddaughters life. He missed me being a mom. He missed his 1st grandson giving him 2 great granddaughters. He missed helping his daughters care for his wife, our mom during her cancer diagnosis and treatment. He missed me growing up from a 22yr old little girl to a 50yr old woman. I missed watching him grow old with Mommy.

Kelly B

I would have missed so much. I would have missed helping my mother navigate Alzheimer's disease. I would have missed my children getting married. I would have missed the births of my 5 grandchildren! My life is so much better than I ever thought it could be.

Sherril

Incredible to think that you have so many nieces and nephews who never got to know you. Your oldest niece graduated high school and is off to college! Three of your nieces and nephews can drive, legally. One nephew carries your name, but you never met him, or his two younger siblings. One nephew has been state football champ, twice! They all would have loved having you cheer them on.

Tiffany
RIP 8/10/2015
In loving memory of Darrin

In 3 1/2 weeks it will be exactly 3 years since I almost would've missed this! I would've missed being there for my oldest daughter bringing her daughter into this world... She would've had to do it without me. I would've missed all the moments with my middle daughter crying on my shoulder as she navigates life as a young adult in college. I would've missed laughing about my youngest daughter & teasing her about how she makes her guardian angels earn their keep bc she somehow managed to drive over 80mph on the INTERSTATE in FIRST GEAR in her little Nissan without blowing the engine up.

When those voices tell you they're better off without you, don't listen... It's all lies. Just hang in there until tomorrow & then hang in there another day!

PM

Had I succeeded in ending my life at fourteen or fifteen, I would have missed the light that eventually appeared at the end of the tunnel—the joy that feels impossible to imagine when your mind is trapped in darkness. I would have missed forming a deep bond with my younger sister and watching her grow into a smart, talented, and beautiful woman. I would have missed standing at my high school graduation, finding my mother in the crowd—a mother who had me at sixteen—and silently telling her, we did it. I would have missed the chance to fall in love with my freshman-year crush and build a life together. Most importantly, I would have missed the clarity that comes with time: the understanding that suicide is a permanent response to a temporary state of mind. Suicidal thoughts convince you that pain is endless, that the worst moments will repeat forever—but that is not the truth. I am here to say there is more life ahead than you can see, and there is light beyond the tunnel.

Briana

Dear Matthew, There are so many moments you have missed that I wish you were apart of. You missed when Josh proposed to me in the ring at a wrestling event. You missed me getting married and sharing a special brother sister dance. You were the one that taught me how to slow dance when we were young kids. I really wish I could've had that moment with you. You missed when I went after my dream of becoming a professional wrestler and tried out for training school. After three years of trying, I finally became pregnant and had my daughter, your niece, May 4th, 2025. She resembles you in some ways. I know you would've absolutely adored her and spoiled her. I would give anything to have you here to share these amazing memories with me. I love and miss you so much. Love, your sister, Marissa.

Marissa
RIP: May 28th, 2019
In loving memory of Matthew

I would have missed myself watch things get better. Fall into place. Still struggle with the depression. But what I couldn't handle before, what I thought wouldn't get better, I overcame. I then would've missed watching my kids grow into amazing adults. My grandchildren come into this world, calling me Nana and falling absolutely in love with me. They can't picture a world without me right now. What more could I ask for right there. Things haven't improved completely for me, but I would've missed a lot outside of just myself because I realize I matter to others.

Donna M

My dad (who took his life in Sept 2024) has missed: my kids' birthdays, my youngest's first day of school and losing his first tooth, my daughter getting her ears pierced, my oldest son getting awards at school for straight A's, me starting my weight loss journey, the new addition to our home, he and my mom's 40th wedding anniversary, his 60th Birthday, and so many more everyday things. If only he would have stayed.

IIC

I aged out of foster care with no family. Hospitalized as a teen a few times for SH and an attempt. I was homeless multiple times until 2023. I was told I could never have kids in 2019. I felt as though if I didn't have a family and I could not make one I had no purpose. All I ever wanted was a baby. Just one at least. I got so desperate I told God, the universe, whatever may be out there that I wouldn't be picky. The baby didn't even have to have all its fingers and toes. Please. Just one.

My daughter was born Oct 9, 2024…and with all fingers and toes.! She lives with me in our apartment that has been in my name since 2023. I work from home for animal healthcare and spend every moment of everyday with her. Those little cheeks, that sweet smile… makes every moment of hell I lived through worth it. I almost didn't get to see it or feel the most amazing love I've ever known. I don't care what happens or who doesn't love me as long as I have her. She is my everything. Having her also broke the generational curse in my family, she will forever have a support system and an amazing grandmother to her kids that I didn't have and the ones before me did not either. I was the last lost child of my family.

Katelyn B

I would have missed my 2 older kids growing up, giving birth to my youngest, becoming best friends with ex-husband, watching my dog live out the rest of his life in content. My Dad, who took his own life in Sept 2024, has missed family dinners, Thanksgiving, Christmas, my Birthday, my kids' Birthdays (he was always the one who lit the candles), the passing of my soul dog (who adored my Dad), and so many more everyday occurrences. I love him and miss him every moment of every day.

V Garcia

You missed raising our three children together, something I was forced to do alone, in my own grief I stumbled doing it alone, but I did it. Watching them graduate high school. Watching our daughter graduate college, she couldnt finish college shortly after you left within months she developed frontal and temporal lobe epilepsy. Her neurologist thinks it could have been from the trauma of that day. We'll never know. It did derail her life. She now has so much happiness the biggest thing for her you missed in her life was you being there to walk her down the aisle when she got married. You missed being here to see our boys grow into men, and our daughter grow into a beautiful woman. For our youngest son missing the biggest part of his life you being in the delivery room when our Grandson came into the world. It was a happiness our family desperately needed. He is missing a lifetime with his Grandfather that you both would enjoyed every minute of. He only knows you from pictures, stories, and visiting your grave, but he knows and loves you. Your missing growing older with me, the plans we had after our children grew up are gone. It's soul crushing having to be here alone. I didn't remarry and won't I couldn't find the kind of love we had. I know your at peace and watching over all of us. I miss not knowing what life could have been for us. I was given 17 years and three beautiful children. I wish you didn't miss them growing into the amazing humans they are today. I have to stop myself from thinking about what could have been if we didn't have to live through the trauma and devastating loss of you, it's to painful to let that thought into my head, even after all these years. You were and you always will be so very much loved and missed.

Kimberly
RIP: 11/06/2002
In loving memory of Jerry

In January of 2019, during the coldest and darkest depths of winter, I had already decided the exact date that my life would end. I wrote my own obituary and chose a date carefully—far enough away from birthdays and holidays that maybe the people I loved wouldn't forever associate those days with my death and would somehow be less upset with me for that. I gave myself one month, just in case something changed. When that day arrived and the weight of the world didn't feel quite so heavy, I just kept going. But, this isn't where my story gets better. Just three weeks later, on February 9, 2019, my father died by suicide. He was only 55. He was the one person in the entire world that I believed truly understood me and the complexity of my heart full of feelings & emotions. He understood the internal battles we both faced and losing him shattered something in me that I still struggle to describe. But in the midst of that grief, I was forced to face a truth I had tried to ignore for years: the same darkness that took his life had been living inside of me too. We carried on as best we could, going through the motions from day to day. Nothing could've ever prepared me for December 14, 2020, when tragedy struck again. My ex-husband, the father of my son died by suicide in the exact same way my father had. Overnight, I became the person responsible for explaining to a five-year-old boy that his daddy was never coming home. The days that followed were filled with grief so heavy it felt impossible to breathe. There were nights I lay on the floor crying until morning and days I forced myself to smile just long enough to get through work. My mind whispered constantly that maybe the world would be better without me too. But every morning my son still needed his mom. Even when I couldn't see hope or a future for myself, I kept choosing to stay for him. In an effort to turn our pain into purpose, I began sharing my story with hopes of raising Suicide Awareness and encouraging others to reach out when they need help.

If I had followed through with the plan I made in January of 2019, I would have missed everything that came after. I would have missed the chance to hold my son while he grieved the loss of his father. I would have missed watching him grow, laugh, and slowly heal. I would have missed discovering that even after unimaginable loss, life can still hold moments of light. My story isn't about having all the answers or about grief magically disappearing. It's about choosing to stay when leaving felt easier. It's about holding space for all of the emotions and giving yourself grace on the hard days. It's about finding your reason to stay and holding on as tight as you can to never let go. Because if I had left this world in 2019, my son would have grown up without both of his parents—and I would have missed the chance to show him that even after the deepest darkness, it is still possible to stay.

Rachel Stikeleather

Pause.
Take a slow breath.
Let your body settle.

GROUNDING PRACTICE

Name today's date.
Name the room you are in.
Name one object in front of you.
Orienting to the present steadies the mind.

JOURNALING & REFLECTION PRACTICE

Take a moment to turn inward.
Let these questions meet you where you are.

What has come before you and what continues through you can be held quietly now, before you begin to reflect.

When you are ready, you are invited to reflect on the threads of time in your own life, at your own pace, in your own way.

1. Who has shaped you across time through presence, memory, or influence and in what ways do you see their imprint in your life today?

2. What qualities, lessons, or people, chosen and unchosen, remain with you across time, and what feels important to carry forward?

Carry forward what feels grounding, comforting and supportive.
Allow everything else to rest and remain here.

DISCOVERING MEANING
AND PURPOSE

"Work (purpose) is love made visible."

Khalil Gibran

Purpose does not always arrive as clarity and a calling. Purpose, meaning, and work often emerge quietly. For some, it grows after surviving. For others, it emerges in the wake of loss. Sometimes it begins as a simple decision to participate in life again, to contribute, to carry forward, to build meaning from what remains.

There are seasons when surviving feels like the only task. And there are seasons when something inside us chooses to try again, not because everything is resolved, but because healing often begins in motion. In learning. In building. In creating. In allowing ourselves to participate in the world once more.

For some, it was returning to a job when getting out of bed felt impossible.

For others, it was raising children while grieving someone who should have been there too.

For some, it was building something new, such as a career, a practice, a calling.

For others, it was simply tending to what was in front of them and choosing not to withdraw from the world entirely.

Purpose does not require certainty. It does not require perfection. It does not require the absence of pain.

It can be found in rebuilding a life after an attempt.

It can be found in living in a way that honors someone who is no longer here.

It can be found in advocacy, in service, in art, in caregiving, in returning to school, in showing up to therapy, to recovery meetings, in surviving another year.

It may look like learning to drive, showing up for a shift, volunteering at a shelter, sitting with someone else in their grief, or simply staying long enough to see what unfolds.

Purpose is not proof that everything is healed. It is often the companion of healing, not its reward.

To engage again, even cautiously, is an act of courage.

Sometimes staying is strengthened by choosing to participate in life again, even when the meaning feels fragile.

It can begin as a single, repeated effort of something chosen, tended, and grown over time. And sometimes it has the chance to grow because you stayed.

My name is Emma and I had thoughts of suicide at the end of 2020. I had just started my senior year of college and amongst roommate complications, my mother (who was battling my uncle's prison habits) had lost her brother to suicide. I was at a point where all my friends were leaving. I was nervous for my future after graduation, and I had no family close by to comfort me. I remember looking at my pills that I used to take daily to help me fall asleep, and thinking to myself about how much I wished I could fall asleep for a long time. I was on anxiety medication, amongst others for various medical reasons, but it wasn't really helping. I'm glad I'm still alive now because not only did I manage to graduate with my B.S., but I also met a ton of really wonderful people who I work with, plus I have some new soon-to-be-sister-in-laws!

I'm not going to lie: life gets really tough sometimes and it's painful when you feel you don't have anyone to comfort you. Life does get better though. Find something you really enjoy, even if it's miniscule. Do you like animals? Find an animal rescue shelter to spend time with some. Do you like writing? Write out a story or characteristics about someone fictional. Maybe you just like to sleep; in that case, listen to something calming. You can do this. I believe in you.

Emma

I would have missed dating the best person I could have ever asked for. I would have missed starting streaming and making absolutely amazing friends from it, some of whom will be lifelong friends. I would have missed graduating college and high school… graduating with my friends. I would have missed watching my parents and sisters grow. I would have missed becoming a chef, proving to people that I am so much more than what they think. To anyone out there struggling, I feel you, and I know you can make it. I made it… and I know you can too. Stay strong, there's people who love you.

Kennedy

I would have missed meeting my other half and best friend all in one. I would've missed letting love back into my life not only for others but for myself. I would've missed healing and realizing there is hope and happiness in the midst of it all. I would've missed being able to caretaker for but also advocate for my autistic daughter. I would've missed her big sisters 8th birthday. I would've missed being able to work in the same school district I grew up in and being able to say that I made it. I would've missed more than anything I could've dreamed and hope for. I would've missed being able to type this and say all this.

Katie

The day I made that choice, I had no vision of a future full of teaching youth, community service, pageantry, modeling, and so much more! When God gives you the strength, endurance, and wisdom to overcome such a deep hole in your heart, you must be willing to share this hope with others. I truly believe that your life could be someone's survival guide to break stigmas and generational curses. I know that if little me had someone such as myself today, she wouldn't have endured a fraction of what she did. I strive to be a beacon for anyone that needs to see beauty, love and grace.

MM

Graduating college Twice!!! Becoming a therapist (LMSW currently) watching my beautiful siblings grow up, my sister is a nurse and has 3 beautiful children!!! Becoming a mother to my sweet daughter, enjoying music, wind in my hair, laughing and laughing and laughing!

Alexis R

Three AMAZING kids!!!

Homeless to home OWNER!!!

Working 7 different jobs to one stable and 2 part time hustles in my field of enjoyment!!

About to publish my first book!

Amazing dog companion!

Wealth is finding ME!

The greatest part of all is the LOVE for life you never knew existed.

Ashton C

I never expected my life to fall apart the way it did. Although I was raised in a very abusive environment, I managed through but when I filed for divorce and primary custody of my two young sons, the legal battle that followed spiraled into something it never should have been – years of unnecessary destruction, false claims, and a system that treated me like I didn't matter. I was a father fighting for his kids, and the process nearly destroyed me. The emotional weight of being erased, doubted, and dragged through something so unfair pushed me to a place I never imagined I'd go. I reached a point where I didn't think I could take one more hit. And I almost didn't stay. But I did. And staying meant I got to see the truth finally come out. Staying meant I got to rebuild. Staying meant I got to be in my sons' lives in the way I always should have been. Staying meant I got to live a life I didn't think I'd ever get back. Today, I work in construction, and I see men carrying different versions of the same silent weight. Pressure. Loss. Divorce. Custody battles. Financial strain. Identity collapse. The things we don't talk about because we think we're supposed to be tougher than the things that are breaking us. I speak now because I know what it feels like to be pushed past the edge by something you didn't deserve and couldn't control. I know what it feels like to think you're out of options. And I know what it feels like to come back. I'm grateful I stayed. I'm grateful for the moments I would have missed. And I'm grateful for the chance to help someone else stay too.

Scott Evans

Hi. I'm Amber. I'm 42 years old. I have many diagnoses, including Borderline Personality Disorder, Bipolar, and PTSD. In my twenties and thirties I attempted suicide eight or nine times. I would have missed so much if I had been successful. In 2018, after I was diagnosed with BPD and was looking for help and support and could find none, I decided to create something myself. I founded a nonprofit organization dedicated to those with BPD, and started running a weekly in-person support group meeting for those with BPD and their loved ones. My support group is the first (and still only) BPD-specific support group in my entire state. I enjoy running my nonprofit and doing everything I can to help others with BPD. Since then, I have founded two more nonprofits, each dedicated to mental health. I also volunteer with NAMI, Emotions Matter, and the NEABPD. And then, about two years ago, I had a revelation and a deep realization. I realized that my life's purpose is to help others. So that is all I have been doing since. I have very deep empathy and consider myself a true altruist. I help people because I don't want people to suffer (like I have). The ONLY reason I help people is to help them. My only intention is to ease their suffering. I believe this is my life purpose, and the reason I will not attempt suicide again. I have to be here. I'm meant to be here. I need to be here—to help others in any way I can.

Amber

I would have missed watching 2 children grow into beautiful young adults. I would have missed the strong relationship I have with my children that has been built over 21 years of breaking cycles, finding joy in small things and laughing together until we cry. I would have missed my recovery and remission from mental illnesses that has allowed me to earn a degree in social work. I would have missed getting to be the adult that younger me needed for the kids I work with. I am so glad I didn't miss the opportunity to love and support so many young people and to see the light of hope flicker behind their eyes. I keep going for the kids I work with and for my friends who didn't get the opportunity to know what they're missing.

Ally

I would have missed my dog, Nala. I would have missed time with my family. I would have missed my marriage flourish. I would have missed the opportunity to give back, so I started a nonprofit organization called Macey's Project. Macey's Project is in honor of my best friend who committed suicide while incarcerated due to her addiction and mental health.

Kelly

My husband died by suicide on June 25, 2009. Our kids were 6 and 8. They are almost 25 and 23 now. He missed their accomplishments. Our kids are so amazing. When Ken died, it was so hard, but my relationship grew with him. He is still part of our lives. He was part of the creation of our family, we shared the same goals and built the foundation for our kids. He was a Dad, a son, a brother, a cousin, a friend, a musician, a psychiatrist, a leader, a compassionate soul, an athlete, so much to us then and even more now. Ken's death does not define us. We are because of you. We use to participate in Kids' Haven: A Center for Grieving Children, now we volunteer.

Barb BG

I am lucky my attempts at suicide were unsuccessful because I've had the privilege of saving others from suicide in both personal and professional life. They wouldn't be here…at least 2 of them…if I hadn't stuck around. I never would have met my incredible husband and adopted our sweet pets. I never would have found out that I could handle college, grad school, and all that has evolved after. I would have missed it all. The name of this page/project had me instantly choked up because death is so final, and I really did almost miss this beautiful existence I'm surrounded by right now.

Katie

There are sometimes moments in my day where I remember my single minded driven decision to take my own life; to leave this earth. The actual day, or really, night was not so much the sole event, like an x marked "here" on a calendar but a culmination of 2 years of angst and the inability to see past my pain any longer. When I read someone's description of a traumatic event, where they talk about time feeling like it's moving in slow motion, and yet also being in the blink of an eye, I think yes! This! Remembering both the goodbye notes that I worked on for weeks, and also the hum of the crickets and the trickling of water from where I lay that night. Big moments and small moments intertwined; feelings of calm mixed with feelings of despair. The fog of those two years and the ocean of tears that I cried seem both so distant and yet still so close. It is in those moments that I find the glimmer of wow, what a miracle that I survived! I had so much to live for. I had a phenomenal husband who'd been my side for 31 years. I had two grown daughters that I was (and am!) immensely proud of; women with a strong sense of social justice and careers in caring and support for others. I had attended the wedding of my youngest months before and had our first grandbaby on the way. I had additional warm and loving family support through my in laws and more friends than I could count on with both of my hands. It was these people who walked beside me as I recovered and who never once blamed me or made me feel guilty for my suicide attempt, and for this I am so grateful. It's hard to put into words everything that I would have missed. The pure love that was shown to me by my family was incredibly healing. The strength of those enveloping hugs and the knowing that I could just be and be loved, gosh, what a gift! I definitely would have missed that. I would have missed the most delightful experience of becoming a Granna. (My daughter said that since my name was Anna, and I would be a grandparent, she wanted me to just add Gr to Anna and thus become Granna!) To hold my newborn grandson and feel his teeny warm body next to mine was a gift I was so unprepared for. Seeing his long blonde eyelashes and running my fingers around his perfectly coiled little ears brought to mind memories of holding my girls as infants, and the rush of love that I instantly felt for them. Those memories and emotions swirled together in a blissful mix of past and present and somehow connected me again to the circle of life, and how amazing it was to still be a part of that infinite circle! I would have missed hearing his precious giggle, and the hugs from his little arms, given with an open mouth sloppy kiss to my cheek. Oh the blessings come rushing at me now! The day we spent apple picking with him, watching Santa clause parade with him, going to the zoo and gazing at his wondering face as he took in otters doing acrobatics in their pond and long necked giraffes staring down at us. Hearing him say "oh yes" when asking if he had fun at daycare and seeing a lot of the ceiling and up his nose as he held the phone, FaceTiming with us! Now we have another little baby grandson, and I marvel again at the soft fuzziness of his dark hair growing in and the adorable deep chuckle he is sharing more and more. I love seeing the differences emerge between the two boys; same parents yet such different genes - our bodies are miracles and watching the baby now giggle at silly antics his brother does. I am aware these gifts are something that not everyone experiences and I'm so very happy that I am a part of this enjoyable grandparent club. I would have missed my other daughter producing and being in that play, and marvelling at her organization, her talent and especially her bravery. I would have missed being asked to help make props. How many people can say they got to cut, glue, stuff and paint 12 chimney sweep brooms! And I most definitely would have missed seeing the final product of such a great musical theatre production. She and I have attended several more large musical theatre shows together, been to see a dinner theatre show this winter with horses and knights, and with my husband are currently counting down the days for trip with the three of us to the UK this spring. I am so aware of how awesome it is to have the opportunity to look forward to things like this. And I'm full of gratitude that I can actually experience the feelings of looking forward to something too. Depression colours everything gray and how beautiful the world is in its bright colours and everlasting optimism! I would have missed the chance to return to the career that feeds my soul; being a nurse. It comes with its own challenges but somehow, this job, this choice, makes me feel that I'm a part of a bigger good, of sharing love, and health and helping others to get back into the world to do their part too. And sometimes, yes, just offering comfort to those who won't be able to return or to those who are losing someone they love. Funny how these moments feel more like a gift to me, than the work that it is intended to be. Sometimes it's powerful to just know that by being an advocate for a patient or another nurse, I am also proving most definitely that I am here and I have much left to offer to this world! Lastly, I am grateful that I didn't have to miss the kind glances from a husband that loves me, his tender kisses and deep hugs and lounging in the hot tub with him, times with my mother knowing she won't be here forever either, hearing her apologize for emotional wounds she committed in the past and our relationship mending as we learn to laugh together again. I would have missed time with my cousins, the sweetest snuggles as the chihuahua who loves me the best turns over for belly rubs and practically smiles at me, and time with my book club sisters; the goofiest and most compassionate women that I know. I would have missed seeing my backyard come alive with greenery and how pretty it looks with the hanging floral baskets in the summer. Seeing the cardinals, chick-a-dees, woodpeckers and blue jays at the bird feeder, and reading a book in the backyard, in the sun, with an iced tea by my side and the blissful chance to just doze off when I get sleepy. Bringing it back full circle, I would have missed sitting by the river, watching the currents take leaves downstream, and seeing the sunlight glistening off the water. Smelling the earthiness of the mud and sitting on a rock with my feet dipped into the cold water. This same river that I chose to be beside for my attempt to take my life, I have now embraced once more and appreciate more than ever that for some reason, I am lucky enough to be here to absorb it's energy and the calm that it brings.

With love and gratitude, Anna P.

Pause.
Take a slow breath.
Let your body settle.

GROUNDING PRACTICE

Inhale slowly.

Exhale fully.

Imagine the exhale loosening tension in your shoulders.

Repeat six times.

JOURNALING & REFLECTION PRACTICE

Take a moment to turn inward.
Let these questions meet you where you are.

Beyond surviving, beyond grieving, we are called forward to find purpose and meaning and to participate in life again, at our own pace and in our own time.

When you are ready, explore what has invited you forward.

1. What has given your life a sense of direction or meaning, whether through rebuilding, caregiving, surviving, honoring someone, or simply continuing?

2. If meaning and purpose feel fragile, where do you notice even the smallest thread of care for yourself, for someone else, in memory of someone you carry, or for something you tend to?

Carry forward what feels grounding, comforting and supportive.
Allow everything else to rest and remain here.

THE BRAVEST THING I EVER DID

"The bravest thing I ever did was rebuilding when I did not even want to live."

John Polo

Rebuilding can look like therapy sessions that stretch you. Recovery meetings that steady you. Medications that help regulate what once felt overwhelming. Boundaries set where there were none. Apologies made. Habits changed. Environments shifted. Patterns interrupted.

For some, rebuilding means learning how to live again after wanting to die. For others, it means learning how to live in a world where someone they love is no longer here.

It can look like attending support groups. Returning to routines. Sorting through belongings.

Raising children through grief. Continuing to show up for birthdays and anniversaries that feel different now. It is not dramatic. It is not always visible. It is often slow.

To rebuild when you did not want to live is a daily act. To continue living when someone else did not is also a daily act. Both require courage.

Rebuilding does not mean forgetting. It does not mean the pain is gone. It means choosing to participate in your own repair or in the repair of your life, even when motivation lags behind commitment. These stories reflect that kind of bravery. Not loud. Not polished. But persistent.

Sometimes the bravest act is simply staying another day.

And another.

And another...

;

I was a 7th grader walking the halls of my school; just like a ton of other young women. Unfortunately, I had a tough home life and was experiencing bullying at a brand new school in a brand new state. This led to my attempt at 12 years old. Now I'm about to turn 23; I have an amazing newly four year old boy who is the light of my life—a degree and a career I passionately work hard for every day. I have my family around me and my friends and my garden I tend too. I would have missed my best friends beating the odds and graduating high school; my mom finding her passion for triathlons and bicycling. My sons first words and his favourite toys. No one tells you how much life can change in 10 years.

Alexia

After a life of abuse and hate I never thought I'd belong anywhere. I never thought I deserved love of any kind whether it be romantic or platonic. When I was in school most kids had goals to go to college and have a career or family; my goal was to be dead by 20. It has been almost three years since my last suicide attempt at 24, and if I had succeeded I would have missed finally having a home, falling in love again, and the birth of my daughter and every bit that came after her arrival from the first time she opened her eyes to her now crawling and saying mama. I would have missed her smiles and her laughs her hugs and snuggles. I would have missed watching the love of my life become a dad and I would have missed myself breaking the circle of abuse I grew up in.

Kat

I would have missed my graduation, learning that recovery from my eating disorder is possible, meeting and being with the one person I truly feel I'm meant to be with, second chances, every friend I've made and life I've touched. Seeing that I can rise up and try again, learn to build a life I love. There is so much that could be said but I'll leave it here.

Travis O

Having 2 nanny kids that changed my life

Finally getting sober for almost 2 months

Finally starting to find things I love to do (addiction steals so much of your time and energy)

Finally learning my struggles are valid and that I'm not just a "lazy horrible person" like I thought for years

Beginning to love myself even when it hurts

Seeing that there is more than one way to live (raised conservative)

Seeing the joy I have the power to bring into the world.

Emma

I've unfortunately been down both roads. I lost my older brother, Alex, to suicide and continue to struggle myself. While our childhood wasn't pretty (and I def was struggling with other things), I didn't start struggling with depression until after the death of my brother. He meant everything to me – was THE person I looked up to. Everything he was, I still want to be. I have yet to meet someone as genuine as Alex. He passed away on my 18th birthday, Feb 1st 2017. He was only 24…Which is nuts considering Im 26 now. If you asked me at 23 if I'd make it to 26, I would have told you no. I was convinced my 25 birthday was going to be too much. To be older than my older brother? Unimaginable. The depression was exactly that. A deep dark soul sucking desire for nothing that quickly turned into suicidal thoughts. I went to work and went to bed. Nothing else. I ate at work. Wore a beany because I could only mentally handle a shower once every week ½. I did nothing. I wanted nothing. I felt nothing, except for when I did…Those were the bad days. This went on for 5 years. Until I looked at my husband (who has stuck by me from age 14 btw—through IT ALL), and couldn't take the guilt anymore. Sorry, this isn't a "and that was that" story. I failed. Hard. Exercise, diet, and every other recommendation on the internet didn't help. I was 2 months into working as hard as I could to feel better and just couldn't anymore. I was worse. The fact that what everyone was saying to do wasn't helping, made the desire to…leave..so much worse. So I went back down. I truly didn't think I'd come back this time. Unfortunately, I grew up with a 'mental health isn't real' family. Mind over matter. Which yes! Great saying for a different situation. However, mental health is more complicated than that. My husband and I decided medication was the next try. It was my last resort. I was terrified. You hear stories about how terrible anti depressants can be. My family gave me hell for it, but I did it anyways. When I say that decision saved my life, I mean it. Don't get me wrong, the first couple I tried were terrible. However, the one I'm on now is amazing. I still have days. That's just how it's going to be once you've had chronic depression, but they are becoming more rare. My range of emotion is now a spectrum! Not just numb or depressed. The day the world was no longer grey, was the day I cried tears of joy for the first time since I lost my brother. Had I done IT the first time I wanted to? It would have been in 2018. I would have missed my wedding. We got married on our 7 year anniversary in 2019. I would have missed seeing my little brother become the amazing man he is today. I'm so proud of him. I deeply miss Alex everyday. I'm so sad we didn't get to experience adulthood together, but I still understand. It's hard to be mad at someone who's only ever done good. However, I will never get him back. There's a hole in my chest that's never going to go away. I wasn't ready to lose my big brother. I still need him every day he's not here. It's common for those who are struggling to feel insignificant and small. Odds are, everyone has someone looking at them the way I looked at Alex. I was quiet about how much I idolized my brother – you might not even know they're there. Everyone's important. Every life matters. My little brother will not lose me like I did Alex. Your friends and family shouldn't lose you either. You mean too much to them.

Heaven

I struggled with a lifetime of abuse, abandonment, assault, and trauma. My first of four attempts was 4/14/07. The last time I considered it was June of 2022. Physically disabled and financially dependent on a physical and sexual abuser. I was waiting on hope for years to be able to leave. I couldn't wait for my financial situation to get better, and my children were watching me whither away to another. I considered for weeks where I'd do it. How I'd do it. Then Naomi Judd lost her battle to these intrusive thoughts – she gave up just before her induction to the Hall of Fame. Her daughter said, "I'm sorry that she couldn't hang on until today." I thought of my babies. I thought "What if the best day of my life isn't too far away?" So I held on. Soon after, I found the courage to get us out of there with a purse, a diaper bag, and probably some loose change in my wallet, at most. We lived in a shelter and then the hotel efficiency we currently live in under a fake name. This has been almost as challenging as living in the abuse. We have now been here for nine months. I laugh every day. I am safe. I am alive. I have two happy and thriving children. I've met someone that showed me how gentle love should be…

And next week…I will be moving in to my own apartment. I see myself waking in the wee hours of the morning, drinking my coffee on my new porch, writing the manuscript of my memoir, while my children sleep in their own bedrooms. The finish line is here. We made it.

I would have missed all of this.

Amanda E

If I had been successful

Because I couldn't deal with the pain of what happened to me at 15, I wouldn't be blessed today as a grown woman with 2 amazing kids and a future that doesn't come easy. But I'm grateful for every sunrise and everything always feels a little better after some sleep. Always sleep on it.

Becca S

My throat was on fire. Be it from the alcohol, tears, or pills that had become lodged, I couldn't tell. I leaned over the toilet bowl again, retching, praying for the pain to end. I had made a mistake, I knew that now. I had children depending on me, children that would walk in and find their mother as they readied themselves for school, alone in a house that did not belong to us anymore, in an environment that had become hostile and violent, a house they had once called home. The home that was now a "grace" to allow the children to ready themselves for school before being cast out again. The numbers in my bank account were red with a sign I had never seen before that the teller had explained meant "negative." But how? I had been saving for years. My children's college fund, life savings, emergency fund, inheritance from my father that had just passed, all gone. He had taken it all. After nine long years of building a life together and a home, we now found ourselves sleeping in my car that was due to be repo-ed in ten short days. Just being laid off two months before, I had no income to top our only shelter, a rusted body sitting on bald wheels, from being taken from us or to put food in our bellies. I counted the pennies on a hungry stomach, making sure theirs were full.

That morning, the one I would have died, I got the phone call. "Could you come in for an interview?" My time was up in the house and I was not permitted to use the facilities that were still in my name. Showering at the gym, I fixed myself up with the best clothes I had that could fit in the garbage bag. Hired on the spot. Two weeks later, pay stub for proof in hand, I met an amazing woman, selling off her joint assets from a cheating man. We resonated and bonded with one another. Rent to own. The papers were signed while we both cried over the turn in our lives. I turned to my second best love in the world, books, and read all I could on using credit, loans, and understanding finance to make it work for us.

Within the month the house was furnished and we had clothes on our backs again. Our walls could not contain the amount of love and joy that we had never known before. There was no yelling, no drinking, no strangers coming and going. Mommy no longer had to work several jobs to support other people, giving us the time to go hiking, to museums, listen to music on full volume while dancing around the kitchen on a floor we owned and cooking food that I didn't have to count pennies for. With love and joy overflowing, we adopted a dog to absorb the extra love we had to give from the happiness we found in stability and freedom. With the spare time, I found myself writing again, set out to become a published author and built a room dedicated to our family's love for art, filled with paintings and drawings we created together. We found home, love, and life that we would have never known, had the pills gone down.

Ashton

I got my classes done finally and go to take my test to get my license back. I have chance back home with me and got us our own place and I've kept the same job 2 1/2 years now. I haven't relapsed even tho it's been super hard and I'm doing everything possible to keep moving up in the world even tho everything inside me just wants to be wherever you are. I miss you the most on the really good days because I wanna tell you about everything good since it was all bad for a while. I love you big brother always and forever I'll be waiting to see you again

Kayla
RIP: 01/04/25
In loving memory of Cj

I can still feel the scissors against my skin as the paramedics cut off my coral colored pajama top. I hear my neighbor saying "Nicole" while slapping my cheek to try to wake me. And then 24 hours later I hear my fathers voice while the nurses gently, yet forcefully shake my body to wake me & take my breathing tube out. It's all so vivid, yet so many details are foggy.

On Monday, November 25, 2019, I tried to take my own life. After years of struggling with anxiety and depression following the death of a boyfriend in 2012, I was put on a mixture of antidepressants which I later found out through a "gene sight" test caused severe suicidal thoughts. I lived in a world of endless psychiatrist visits, medications, inpatient stays, surgeries, an addiction, pain & deep internal sadness. Exactly one year ago today is the day that I now refer to as "My reborn day."

Once I had regained my health, I realized that I had to make a decision. I could no longer let anger, sadness, depression and medication dictate the path of my life. If I was to move forward and truly overcome these obstacles, I must make the declaration that I am in control of my destiny, and me alone. I would no longer be a slave to these thoughts that formerly controlled my life. I made the decision that I wanted to live and only could do what was necessary to take these steps. No one could do it for me. I appreciated the support of my family and friends but their words and encouragement would mean nothing if I didn't have the drive and desire in my own heart.

I found a job. It wasn't my dream job but it gave me a sense of purpose and accomplishment. I began taking the necessary steps to move away from my parents home because I knew that in order to beat this illness I needed to do it on my own. I saved money and got myself an apartment, a car, and the things I needed to be on my own. The feeling of independence in my heart was more therapeutic than you could ever imagine. I was beginning to feel self worth and seeing myself the way others have always seen me. For once in my life, I was believing in myself. From here on, things starting going in my direction and it was all because I had faith in myself.

My journey does not stop here. I have accomplished more this year than I have in my entire life. I have become such an independent, happy, reliable woman in just a years time and I could not express how proud I am of myself. I have stopped taking all medication that was so easily fed to me when I said the word "anxiety". I changed my career path & enrolled in school to help further my education. I have let go of any negativity and have grown as a person. Life is not promised and I gave up, but my body didn't. THAT is all the proof I need that I am meant to be here.

The amount of gratitude I feel to be alive is unmeasurable. Some would say "I wish I could take it back", yet for me, to get to where I am present day I wouldn't change any of it. This was and is my story and I wouldn't feel so protected, so joyous, so free spirited and ALIVE had I not struggled. I am thankful for the past because it led me to the woman I became in a years time, a warrior!

My heart is full knowing that even one person will benefit from my story. It is my priority to make people happy, spread positivity and show others I am living proof IT WILL GET BETTER. No matter the obstacle you are facing, YOU WILL GET THROUGH IT.

So if no one has told you, I will. I am PROUD OF YOU. The world needs you, your smile, your intelligence and your strong will. Always forgive yourself for a bad day even a bad decade. Start and end each day with gratitude. Be thankful for blessings we often take for granted. The only person you should look up to is the person you will become.

Remember, in order to love who you are, you cannot hate the experiences that shaped you.

If I can, you can. Let me show you.

Nicole Belfiore — Survivor - Advocate

I would have missed years of sobriety, a college degree, an amazing partner, and a beautiful little girl. I am so glad I wasn't successful. My life is beautiful today!

Alisha

I am one of many who suffer from PTSD and with that Anxiety and Depression. I have been suffering for many years and this has had a tremendous effect and impact on not just my life, but my children, as well as friendships, its had a severe impact on my quality of life and health. This is my story, its what I call – "The Forgotten Battle."

I hail from a long and proud military family. I served in the Royal Australian Air Force. I feel privilege and I'm proud to have served this great Nation both on Australian soil and on overseas Operations. However, that service came with a personal price. My story of the Black Dog surfaced not by my choice, but triggering events. I didn't wake up one morning changed, this change has been happening over a period of many years. Added to this, my wife of 45 years marriage/partner decided that after several known affairs, which we let go, she decided to leave me for her older business partner, in January 2024. She admitted to me that she had been in an affair with him for quite a number of years and she showed no remorse. My marriage of abuse is another story, but forms a big part of my suicidal situation. Thankfully, I'm now divorced and out of a toxic DV abusive relationship.

All this finally pushed me to the breaking point, where I was ready to give up. I was ready to end my life, in fact I had planned it so it would look like a workplace accident. It was at this point that I was admitted to a Mental Health Hospital. I didn't realise it at the time, but this was the turning point in my life, the turning point that I needed. Sad to think it came to that before I got help, but I got help. It was then through ongoing counselling and therapy groups, that I started to understand and accept what had been happening to me. It was a realization, an awakening that the time had come for me to take a stand and fight back. If I allow myself some self-praise, some self-love, over the last 24 months ive achieved so much and this includes, accepting my emotional health for what it is and the fact that Im now happier and my overall health is on a great path. Lets stop using the word 'mental health', its such a harsh and old school word, its like a door slamming in your face, it implies that Im broken or defective, well Im not. Emotional health is a softer more accepting word, after all are not in a world that supports compassion and respect, inclusion and acceptance. Please include me, not segregate me. Im a very healthy and tone 95kgs and a lot fitter both in body and mind. Im getting more comfortable talking with people. Ive learnt the excitement of the art of conversation, where its often said you cant shut me up. As for leaving my house, Im rarely at home. Im either at the gym, or out doing some form of other social activity. Im now happier on my own, I am no longer controlled or suppressed, nor do I live in fear of threats of anger. I have my independence back and I can refocus on my initial emotional health issues. Taking my life back to reclaim what is mine. Buying my first home and moving into my own forever home, Ive learnt to make decisions on my own, Ive bought a new car. Ive formed new friendships, Ive got a new truly loving girlfriend, Ive even been able to reconnect with my older brother and sister, nephews, of which I hadn't spoken with for some 20 years.

Im loving life and Im pleased that Im still here to enjoy it, to make new memories. Im now enjoying my life, not my new life, but my life, you see, the person you see in front of you, has always been here, the cheeky me, the Monty Python, John Cleese, Mr Bean that some of you have started to see. Ive learnt to show and feel emotions, which is a wonderful feeling. My emotional health issues have just suppressed me for far too long, but now in the words of John Newton who penned the words to Amazing Grace, I once was lost, but now I am found. Ive not only crawled my way through the rubble, been to hell and back in a washing machine, but now Im gaining my balance to stand firm on high ground, life can throw me to the wolves, but know this, I have returned, leading the pack.

Don't think that you are mended overnight, or that you are magically cured, you're not, what Im saying is, at times, yes, it is really hard work, I still have my different days, where I need a lot of energy and planning to achieve the simple things. Im still dealing with some personal issues which I accept I will never get an ending or closure, but, its ok to accept, that Im not able to accept some things or get answers. Im still learning, that recovering from emotional health is difficult, but it's not impossible. No-one can make you forget what happened, the secret, is to learn how to live with it, that in itself is acceptance. I want to show you that with the right help, faith and believing in yourself, you can recover your emotional health and live a happy and content life. You've just need to want it. So that's what I have done or achieved, BUT, what life's lesson have I learnt??? Ive learnt that when you talk you are only repeating something you already know. But, if you listen you may learn something new. These following words are not all mine, Ive adapted them to suit me and the life lesson and this is my message to you that I want to nail home…..
The biggest lie we are ever told is often the one we tell ourselves every morning in the mirror, we say we are fine when our spirit is screaming for help, constructing a reality where our pain doesn't exist. We build these walls not to keep others out, but to trap in our own broken pieces. In that self-composed isolation, we take on the impossible task of being our own rescuers. But let me tell you a truth that you need to hear, trying to heal all by yourself is one of the heaviest burdens you will ever carry. Your silent battles do not make you weak, they make you a warrior, but even the strongest of warriors will eventually need their armour attended to by another's hand. Your healing was never meant to be a lonely secret. Letting someone see your scars is the first

step to truly letting the light in. Just one small positive thought in the morning can change your whole day. Because if a problem can be solved, there's no need to worry, and if it can't be solved, worry is of no use.

Everyone has a story and this is my story.

Ian

My beautiful family and two kids. Knowing that you really don't HAVE to hate yourself, no matter how much or how long you have been…

Tara

You have missed your young children growing...learning to ride a bike, playing in the pool we had bought for you & the kids, watching your baby girl crawl, then walk & now starting to say words. You missed your best friend coming to Maine to follow through with your plans to get each other's kids together and see them bond and play. You missed your baby's first birthday. Did you know I would cry everyday since you left? Did you not know how loved you were by so many people that knew you beyond your family & friends? Learning to live life without you feels so unbearable, but knowing this pain is not anything I would want another person to bare. You were & still are so precious to us & I will look for signs of your spirit in your children & the things we do to honor & remember you. You ARE Forever missed, forever loved & always in our broken hearts.

Sandy
RIP: 04/25/2024
In loving memory of Kaleigh

what i would've missed had i not seen the view from halfway down. the pain you felt when you saw my scars. the shame you felt when i told you. i would've missed all of the horrible things that have happened since. the wrecks, the hospitals, the deaths, the meds. the winters, the fires, the work, the sleds. had i not seen life from its very edge, i would've missed this pain. i would've missed this peace. the hope in your eyes, as i said, "I do!" the joy in your voice as i opened the door i would've missed all of the happiest moments of my life since then. the kids, the house, the toys, the books the colors, the love, the hugs, the looks had i not seen this, from the very edge of death, i would've missed my very best.

Nova

Pause.
Take a slow breath.
Let your body settle.

GROUNDING PRACTICE

Sit comfortably, with your feet resting on the floor if possible.

Gently press your feet into the ground.

Notice the contact.

Notice the support beneath you.

Take one slow breath in through your nose.

And a slow breath out through your mouth.

Say quietly to yourself:

I am here.

I have endured.

In this moment, I am safe.

Take one more slow breath.

When you are ready, continue.

JOURNALING & REFLECTION PRACTICE

Take a moment to turn inward.
Let these questions meet you where you are

Whether your courage has looked like rebuilding or simply continuing, let that truth be enough for now.

When you are ready, you may reflect on the bravery within your own story.

1. What is something you have lived with, rebuilding or continuing that required more courage than you gave yourself credit for?

2. If bravery feels difficult to see in yourself, what small act of staying, past or present, might quietly reflect your strength?

Carry forward what feels grounding, comforting and supportive.
Allow everything else to rest and remain here.

WHAT HAVE I BEEN DOING THESE DAYS? HEALING

"What have I been doing these days, you wondered.

I didn't answer you with my words, with excuses, defensiveness, redirection, or a, "not much",

like I have done so many times before.

Instead, I showed you the scars as evidence of the work I have done to mend the places where history had once broken and wounded me.

I let you see the quiet peace that followed, breath by breath, step by step, reorienting a mind and body that once only knew how to brace for trauma and harm.

I did not hide the grief either. It sits as a welcomed companion beside the healing now, no longer swallowing me whole.

And then I sat in stillness, because I have found grace in a mind that can rest.

What have I been doing these days? Healing--that is what I have been doing."

Julie A Rocco

Healing does not arrive all at once. It unfolds in decisions to keep appointments, take medication, if needed, to practice breathing when the body tightens, to ask for help when old patterns urge silence. For some, it also unfolds in the decision to attend the memorial, to sort through belongings, to honestly answer the question of how you are doing when the answer is complicated.

Some days it looks like progress. Some days it looks like maintenance. Some days it simply looks like not going backward. For those living with loss, some days it looks like carrying memory and grief without being consumed by it.

There are moments when the past feels close. When thoughts return. When the ache resurfaces. When exhaustion surfaces. Healing does not erase those moments. It changes how you meet them. It creates space between impulse and action. It creates space between memory and collapse. It builds strength in the pause.

Staying does not mean the struggle disappears. It means learning how to move through it without surrendering to it. For those grieving, staying may also mean learning how to remain in a world that feels altered, and how to love someone who is no longer physically present.

To be here now, aware, breathing, reflective, is not accidental. It is the result of effort, support, practice, and choice. Not once. But many times. Over and over. Sometimes it is the choice to stay. Sometimes it is the choice to keep going after someone else could not.

It is about staying, even when you do not see the whole path. It is about taking the next step anyway. It is about allowing life, in whatever form it now holds, to continue.

It is about a commitment, "I will see you tomorrow."

When I think about what I would have missed, it goes far beyond anything I could imagine. I would have missed watching my children grow up, their first days of school, their personalities, the joy of seeing them become their own people. I would have missed becoming a peer support specialist, something that has given my life purpose and allowed me to help others in ways I never imagined. I would have missed healing so much of the trauma I once carried I would have missed rebuilding a healthier relationship with my mom, something that took time, honesty, and growth. I also would have missed the spiritual growth I've experienced, the comfort I've found in God, the peace that comes from feeling guided, supported, and grounded in something bigger than myself. And I would have missed learning what healthy connection feels like. I would have missed the life I have now, a life I couldn't have pictured back then. And I know there are still so many beautiful things ahead of me that I haven't even discovered yet but im so ready for.

Karina Ramos

He did miss. His sorrows and despairs were too much. He thought this was his act of love. But his absence created a wound so large that bumping it, even after years of healing, will have it bleeding again. He missed my mom remarrying a man that hurt me. I never told her because of how hurt she was by your leaving. I didn't want to be responsible for another one gone.

He missed my first heartbreak, and all the ones following thereafter. He never got to teach me about the difference between a good and a bad guy. He missed my first serious partner and us buying our first home. He missed me staying with a man who bought hookers. He missed me betraying myself for a man I loved. He missed me almost following in his footsteps. Then I remembered everything he missed, and how it caused me to feel. Then I remembered my mom. Every time his missing presence screamed, she screamed louder. I would have missed her driving two hours away to immediately help me move out when I was ready. I would have missed her cheering me on as I found my new tribe. I would have missed hearing her tell me how worried she was for me and how happy and proud of me she is for finding myself again. I would have missed my mom watching me heal my wound into a scab. It can still bleed here and there, but the blood is a beautiful reminder of what I didn't miss.

Katie

What would I have missed? I think about this often, when I think about how someone I knew in middle school had tragically ended their life. I was also dealing with my own mental health issues, and had thoughts of ending my life. It's now been 10 years since and when you're that young you truly don't believe other people when they say that your life will change. So…what would I have missed? I would have missed discovering who I am, my sexuality and gender identity. It wasn't the most joyous experience all the way around, especially in terms of acceptance, but I can say I'm proud of myself for being authentic, and I will never let someone take that away from me. It was also more than just those two parts.

I spent a lot of time trying to please others, and it wasn't until I entered adulthood that I began to explore who I was and what I really liked. I found music that no matter how many times I play it, I experience joy. I found a love for art, digital and on paper. I found I love cooking genuinely, and if you come over, expect to be over fed. I finally found enjoyment of literature through audiobooks (too many bees in my head to read books, can't absorb a thing) and now I enjoy all those books I wanted to read but found to daunting to. I would have missed finishing college when I was told I wasn't smart. I might have ADHD and a processing speed disability but dammit! I did it! I honestly never thought I would live that long to say I graduated college.

I would have missed meeting the love of my life. The person I want to grow my life with. He too struggled with his own past, and we work together everyday to build a better life for ourselves. He's my teammate. I feel safe. I feel supported. I would have missed creating a connection with another person, a connection at the time I was never able to conceptualize. I never thought I could be in a relationship with another human the way I am with my partner.

I would have missed the chance to find my passion. The work I do can be emotionally draining, and heartbreaking, but then there's also the times I can make who I am working with smile, and help them through some of the toughest stuff that no one should have to go through. I make sure to let them know they aren't alone. I don't want them to feel the way I felt.

I brought up a lot of big moments so far but there's also just tiny moments, that may be small but doesn't mean they aren't important. The small moments: Staying up till 2am with friends giggling and playing cards. Enjoying the quiet summer day as I fish (nap) on the lake. Buying all those silly things I wanted as a kid but could never afford, but am now an adult with a kid brain and adult money. Staying up till 4am talking about life with the love of my life cuddling in bed. Being able to afford spoiling my dog rotten. Finally seeing the Supernatural finale and my boys finally being able to rest (don't you cry no more) Feeling moments of genuine joy and laughter. Forming the best group of gay/neurodivergent friends I could ever ask for. Hearing someone call me a professional – I'm a baby in a suit y'all. Being able to travel, and that's only just begun.

Well if I can summarize the last 10 years of my life it wasn't unicorns farting rainbows, in fact there was a lot of pain for the better half of that 10 years, but I experienced it. I was still here to experience it all. There was a lot of bad but there also was a lot of good. There was and is a lot of love that surrounds me. I think about the child who ended their life when I was in middle school and I weep thinking about what she missed. I will hold her memory in my heart, and experience it for us both. Today, I still have my battles, there's good and bad days as I've said, and sometimes negative thoughts tend to resurface. I remind myself how much love and support is in my corner. I remember all the plans I still have, and how much more I still have yet to do. I think about how much more I could help others in my life. So if anyone reads this, you're not alone, and I send the largest hug imaginable. You are worthy of happiness, you are worthy of love, you are worthy of kindness. You've got this, reach out, keep fighting.

Ty

The past 2 years since my attempt have been a whirl wind. I went on my dream trip to the beach and saw my favorite animal in person for the first time (sea turtles) and made all kinds of memories with my family. I've gone back to school to pursue my dream job of being an art teacher and I'm officially president of the school's art club. I got a part time job at an art school (I never thought I'd work again). I got a dog and she has saved my life countless times and is the light of my life. I've rediscovered myself and got on the right meds so I'm now free from the fog of depression for the first time in the last 12 years. I'm healing from my trauma little by little. And most importantly, I am finding joy in the little things of everyday life. I've found my faith again. I've been to every birthday and anniversary party I can possibly go to. I'm embracing life for what it is finally and it is BEAUTIFUL. I went from hating life to loving every day life has to offer. I am living proof that it does get better! Life can be so beautiful and realizing that is what I would have missed the most.

Rhylee

I first realized I was depressed around age 14 although looking back it started at 12. I moved half way across country leaving everything behind to help care for my dying grandfather. I lost family and friends and fell into a deeper depression and became suicidal. My first attempt was at 15. Then again at 16 and 18. I made no plans for my future as I was so certain I would have succeeded at 18. I smoked tobacco and marijuana, drank, self harmed, anything I could do to make the pain stop. At 22 I no longer self harming and decided it was time to better myself. I had to train myself to think happy thoughts and still slack, I stopped smoking and drinking at 23. Ive met the love of my life and we have 3 cats together. Ive been sober for close to 2 years. Im almost 25 now.

Allyson

I would have missed the chance to find myself and to discover that there truly is good within the bad. I wouldn't have been able to excel in my career, behavioral health field, and helped others the same way I needed help. I wouldn't get to see my little brother grow up and become the amazing athlete that he is. I still struggle. Everyday. But I feel content and I prioritize my health. I surround myself with those who understand me and listen and love me for who I am. There is a little bit of good in every day, we just have to look for it sometimes.

Katilyn

What I would have missed.....The joy and love of my family on my special day. The birth, and growth of my loved ones over the years. Bonding time every holiday with my family. The improvements I made in my life. I couldn't imagine the hurt and tears I would've brought if I stayed silent...I'm proud of myself for staying strong and overcoming my trials and tribulations. If I dare to ever reach that point of darkness again, I will think about what I wouldve have missed if I left ;

Courtney

What you have missed since leaving. So much more than I could ever write. You've missed possibly finding the true love of your life and having children of your own. Missing the chance to become a better father than the one that we had. You've missed the opportunity to fulfill my lifelong dream of becoming an Auntie. And even to this day, I truly miss knowing that I never will be called "Auntie". You've missed two amazing nephews and a niece who grew up to be the most wonderful humans. And the opportunity to teach and help nurture them while they grew. You've missed two great nephews and a great niece who would have brought so much light into you dark life.

You've missed moving to Texas where you would have hated the heat as much as I do. But you also missed the years of horses, cows and endless trail rides that lasted for days. Camping under the stars, fishing and hunting endlessly. You've missed finishing our plans to move to Alaska. We could have achieved it. Together. A shared dream that never held the same meaning, after you left. So I couldn't find it in my heart to pursue a dream I shared with you. without you. You have missed devastating losses and grief. Grief, at times, I didn't think I would be able to endure. And somehow have.

However you have missed the love and happiness of spending the final years with Papa. You missed those years with him and all of his shenanigans. You missed so much laughter and joy with the one person who never let us down. as well as Mom and Auntie. The discovery of an entire native historical village on Auntie's property. Mom's near sobriety and the happiness she found being a grandmother. You missed driving the back country roads in a pickup truck, with a dog at your side, probably hunting illegally. Because of course we would have.

You have missed growing old right behind me. And laughing with me, and at me through all *what the heck now* moments. Most of all, you have missed a lifetime of love from your big sister. A love so strong and deep, that no amount of time or space between us will ever erase. You were my first *child* from the day they brought you home from the hospital. All pink, wrinkly and hungry. And out of everything that you have missed, I pray you've found the peace that you could never find in this world. The peace that puts together all the broken pieces. Aloha Nui

Kat
RIP: 12/23/1988
In loving memory of Jack

Oh…so much. I would have missed my kids growing up. Missed my older 2 graduate. Missed record snow in my hometown in Florida last year. Would have missed my second chance at life. Would have missed feeling I finally belong to a family.

Aimee

I would've missed going back to school. I would've have missed finally making progress with my mental health. I would've missed finally standing up for myself. I would've missed a job that believes in me. I would've missed the "it can get better". I'm thankful I didn't miss these things even though I thought I wanted to.

Sarah JK

Learning that I could be a good mom, despite my lacking example.

Learning that someone can love me as I am.

Learning that I am worthy.

And learning that I like me. And even if I were the only one, that's enough.

Cassie

I would've missed my healing, my older son's graduation, my college graduation, my younger son getting his driver's license, my daughter learning the euphonium, saying goodbye to my grandmother as she crossed over....i would have missed so much.

Jodi

I would have missed meeting the love of my life and experiencing a love I have never had, I would have missed having my son (who is now 6) and not known what it felt like to be a mother! The love I have for my child is the deepest most pure love I have ever felt. I wake up everyday being so thankful I gave myself another chance. My baby is my world and just looking in his eyes or having him lay next to me, watching him grow, brings me a joy I would have never experienced nor known even existed. I wouldn't have the home I have, the wonderful job I have now, or the new mindset that I can do anything I put my mind to.

I look back to the time when I thought I couldn't go on another day and realized...I DID IT, I made it! And it made me open my eyes and made me went to challenge myself to do all the things I thought I would never do! I push myself every day to do things I always said I wouldn't, because I now know, if I put my mind to it, I CAN! My goal now is to be the best mother I can be and to always remind my son how loved and valued he is and how his life has meaning and purpose, so that he doesn't struggle like I did. My goal is to supply him with all the love and wisdom my life once lacked. He is my purpose now.

Sabrina

I lost my 24 year old son last December. Since his passing his son has started pre K. And he just turned 4. He's missed a birthday. He would've been 25. Mostly he's missed all the love my mommy heart has for him. If you are struggling you can talk to me. You're story isn't over yet. Please just stay.

Mary
RIP: 12/21/23
In loving memory of Damian

I would have missed my graduation. Meeting and knowing my son. And most importantly seeing myself get better finally.

Krow S

I would have missed the peace that I finally found in myself.

Harlee

Pause.
Take a slow breath.
Let your body settle.

GROUNDING PRACTICE

Place your hand on your chest.
Say quietly:
"For this moment, I am here."
Take one breath.
Then another.
Pause. Rest. Return to breath.

JOURNALING & REFLECTION PRACTICE

Take a moment to turn inward.
Let these questions meet you where you are.

Healing does not mean forgetting. It means grief no longer defines the entire landscape.

Healing is not dramatic. It is daily.

Breath by breath.

Choice by choice.

Day by day.

It is about staying, even when when you do not see the whole path. It is about taking the next step anyway.

When you are ready, reflect on what healing looks like for you now.

1. What does healing look like in your life right now, not in theory, but in practice?

2. As you continue your healing, what might your future self thank you for?

Carry forward what feels grounding, comforting and supportive.
Allow everything else to rest and remain here.

STATISTICS AND INSIGHTS

Stories allow us to feel the human experience. Stories show the soul. Statistics reveal its reach. Statistics show the scale.

Both matter.

One speaks in voice. The other in numbers.
Together, they deepen our understanding.

Suicidal suffering is often framed as an individual crisis. Yet no life exists outside of context. Access to care, cultural silence, financial instability, trauma, discrimination, and policy decisions all shape who receives support and who does not. These stories reflect both personal experience and the environments that surround it.

Suicide is both deeply personal and profoundly widespread. It affects individuals, families, classrooms, workplaces, and communities across every demographic. While stories illuminate the lived reality of survival and loss, data helps us understand the scope of what so many carry often quietly and without recognition.

The numbers, both in scope and scale, that follow are not included to alarm, but to inform. They remind us that suicidal thoughts, attempts, and losses are not rare or isolated experiences. They are part of a larger public health reality that calls for compassion, conversation, and accessible care.

Behind every statistic is a life. Behind every number is a name, a family, a story.

Understanding the magnitude does not replace the humanity. It strengthens our resolve to respond to it. When we comprehend the pervasiveness, we begin to recognize why conversation, access to care, community, and compassion are not optional. They are essential.

Every life holds impact beyond what can be measured.

Every story you have just read and every number listed here is evidence of that.

THE SCOPE

- Suicide remains one of the leading causes of death in the United States.
- Hundreds of thousands of people each year report seriously considering suicide.
- Public health surveys suggest that a substantial proportion of the population experiences suicidal thoughts during their lifetime.
- Public health data suggest that attempts and ideation far exceed deaths
- Each suicide loss deeply impacts surviving family members, friends, colleagues, and communities.

Suicide is a leading cause of death worldwide. It affects people in every country, across income levels and cultures.

Suicide does not discriminate, but access to care, stigma, systemic inequities, and social isolation often determine who receives support and who does not.

Sources: Centers for Disease Control and Prevention (CDC); American Foundation for Suicide Prevention (AFSP); Substance Abuse and Mental Health Services Administration (SAMHSA); World Health Organization (WHO), most recent available data.

WHO IS IMPACTED

No single demographic owns this pain.

Suicide affects people across every stage of life, from adolescents navigating identity and belonging, to adults balancing caregiving, work, and invisible pressure, to older adults facing isolation, illness, or accumulated loss.

It touches:

- Young people experiencing bullying, social exclusion, academic pressure, or online harm
- College students navigating transition, independence, and uncertainty
- Parents and caregivers carrying financial strain or generational responsibility
- Middle-aged adults facing career instability, divorce, health concerns, or role shifts
- Older adults coping with chronic illness, bereavement, or diminished mobility

It also disproportionately impacts individuals living at the intersection of vulnerability and systemic inequity, including:

- Veterans and active military personnel
- LGBTQ+ individuals, particularly transgender youth
- People living with chronic pain or long-term medical conditions
- Individuals with substance abuse challenges
- Survivors of abuse, assault, or childhood trauma
- People experiencing housing instability or financial insecurity
- Individuals involved in the criminal legal system

- Rural communities with limited access to mental health care
- Communities of color navigating systemic barriers and cumulative stress

Men die by suicide at higher statistical rates. Women report higher rates of attempts and suicidal thoughts. Nonbinary and transgender individuals experience significantly elevated risk.

Suicide loss survivors, parents, siblings, partners, children, friends, also carry increased vulnerability and are at increased risk for depression, complicated grief, and suicidal thoughts. Grief after suicide carries unique complexity including shock, guilt, anger, unanswered questions, and stigma.

Understanding these patterns is not about categorizing pain. It is about recognizing where support must be strengthened.

Sources: CDC; AFSP; National Institute of Mental Health (NIMH); The Trevor Project; American Association of Suicidology (AAS).

CONTRIBUTING FACTORS

There is rarely one single cause.

Suicide risk often develops through the interaction of:

- Depression and other mood disorders
- Anxiety disorders
- Trauma and PTSD
- Substance use
- Social isolation
- Relationship loss or conflict
- Legal or financial stress
- Access to lethal means
- Feelings of hopelessness or burdensomeness
- Untreated mental health conditions
- Cultural or generational stigma around seeking help

For suicide loss survivors, risk may also be shaped by:

- Survivor's guilt
- Repetitive intrusive thoughts
- Unresolved questions
- Social withdrawal
- Fear of further loss

Suicidal crises often occur during periods of acute stress combined with limited perceived options.

What feels permanent in the moment is often temporary in reality but the nervous system cannot always distinguish the difference without support.

Sources: Contributing risk factors reflect research identified by the CDC, NIMH, and WHO.

PROTECTIVE FACTORS

Research consistently shows that suicide risk decreases when individuals experience:

- Strong social connection
- A sense of belonging
- Cultural or community support
- Access to mental health care
- Skills in emotional regulation
- Reduced access to lethal means
- Reasons for living -- large or small
- Meaningful roles or responsibilities
- Experiences of being heard and validated

Protective factors do not eliminate struggle.
They create buffers against it.
Sometimes protection looks dramatic.
Often, it looks ordinary.
A text message.
A therapy appointment kept.
A pet waiting at home.
A night out with a friend.
A volunteer activity.
A morning routine.
A promise made for today.

Sources: Protective factors reflect suicide prevention research identified by the CDC, WHO, and NIMH.

TREATMENT AND RECOVERY

Suicidal thoughts are treatable.

Evidence-based treatments include, but are not limited to:

- Cognitive Behavioral Therapy (CBT)
- Dialectical Behavior Therapy (DBT)
- Medication management
- Trauma-informed therapy
- Grief-specific therapy for suicide loss survivors
- Peer support groups
- Crisis stabilization services

Medication, when appropriate and monitored, saves lives.

Therapy builds skills.

Connection restores perspective.

Healing is not linear.

Relapse does not equal failure.

Recovery may require multiple attempts at care.

It is common for individuals to need time to find the right therapist, the right medication, or the right support structure.

Asking for help is not a weakness. It is a strategy to save your life or that of someone you know.

Sources: Evidence-based treatment approaches are supported by research from the American Psychological Association (APA), NIMH, and the Suicide Prevention Resource Center (SPRC).

A NOTE ON WARNING SIGNS

While not all suicidal crises are predictable, warning signs can include:

- Talking about wanting to die
- Expressing hopelessness
- Withdrawing from others
- Giving away possessions
- Sudden mood changes
- Increased substance use
- Searching for lethal means

For suicide loss survivors, warning signs may also include:

- Intensified grief around anniversaries
- Heightened guilt or self-blame
- Avoidance of previously meaningful relationships
- Increased rumination about the death

Early intervention matters.

Sources: Warning signs adapted from guidance by the CDC and NIMH.

DATA AND RESOURCES INFORMED BY

National and international public health reporting, including the Centers for Disease Control and Prevention (CDC), National Institute of Mental Health (NIMH), World Health Organization (WHO), Substance Abuse and Mental Health Services Administration (SAMHSA), American Foundation for Suicide Prevention (AFSP), American Association of Suicidology (AAS), The Trevor Project, and the Suicide Prevention Resource Center (SPRC).

Data has been drawn from national and international public health reporting most recent available data at time of publication. Resources are highlighted to help guide individuals toward help and offer direction. This is not an exhaustive list, but it may offer you a place to begin as you reach out for support, while also recognizing there are many unique forms of help someone may require.

RESOURCES
IF YOU OR SOMEONE YOU KNOW NEEDS IMMEDIATE SUPPORT

If you are in the United States:

- Call or text 988 (National Suicide & Crisis Lifeline)
- Chat via 988lifeline.org
- In an emergency, call 911

If you are outside the U.S.:

- Visit the International Association for Suicide Prevention (iasp.info/resources/Crisis_Centres/) for country-specific crisis lines.

For suicide loss survivors:

- Alliance of Hope (allianceofhope.org)
- American Foundation for Suicide Prevention (afsp.org)

If calling feels overwhelming, consider texting.

If texting feels overwhelming, consider sitting beside someone and asking them to call with you.

You do not have to carry crisis alone.

DEAR ONE WHO IS STILL HERE

These pages carry courage. Not because every story resolves neatly, but because each one was offered honestly. Some stories are still unfolding. Some remain tender. Some are carried in memory. All of them matter.

If you are a suicide ideation survivor or suicide attempt survivor, your presence here is not small. Staying, especially when staying felt impossible, is no ordinary act.

If you are a suicide loss survivor, your grief is held here. The love you carry did not disappear when the life of your loved one ended. It continues in the ways you remember, in the questions you still hold, and in the life you are learning to live alongside that loss.

If you find yourself somewhere in between, found in struggle, in questioning, in quiet endurance, you belong here too.

This book was not created to fix what cannot be easily resolved. It was created to hold space for truth, imperfection, and complexity and to honor lived experiences as they were shared by suicide ideation, attempt, and loss survivors.

We cannot heal what we are not allowed to name. And naming, even when it is messy or incomplete, is an act of courage.

If something in these pages stirred grief, hold it with compassion.

If something stirred hope, keep it close.

If something stirred recognition, lean into it.

You do not have to resolve everything today.

You do not have to know the entire path ahead.

Sometimes the bravest act is simply staying another day, and another, and another.

Thank you for staying with these stories.

Thank you for staying in whatever way you are able.

You have reached the final pages, but this is not an ending.

It is my hope that within these stories you found moments of connection, meaning, and perhaps even healing and something you can hold onto as you move forward.

There are moments waiting for you. There are moments you do not want to miss.

Much love,
Julie

The conversation continues.

If these pages stirred something in you, let it be the beginning, not the end.

If you need support, reach out.

Call someone. Text someone. Sit with someone.

Help is not weakness. It is connection in motion.

If this book offered you language for something hard to name, consider sharing it with someone who may need it too. Stories travel farther than we do.

If you would like to contribute your own *What I Would Have Missed* story, you are invited to use this QR Code or visit: www.whatiwouldhavemissed.com.

If you would like to share your reflections and feedback on this
book, you are invited to use this QR Code or visit:
www.whatiwouldhavemissed.com.

ACKNOWLEDGEMENTS

This book exists because many people trusted me with their words, their memories, and their lived experience.

I am deeply grateful to those who shared reflections for What I Would Have Missed. Your willingness to name moments of survival, loss, love, and absence make these pages possible. Thank you for allowing your stories to be held with care, compassion, and dignity.

I also extend my gratitude to the clinicians, researchers, advocates, and community leaders whose work continues to shape how we understand suicide ideation, attempt, and survival, and suicide loss with greater compassion, clarity, and responsibility.

To my partner, friends, and family members who supported this work quietly and consistently, thank you for your steadiness, patience, and belief in what this book could offer.

To Chandler for helping to design a book that holds the full truth of those who shared their stories while also making space for the reader to be held compassionately. To St Petersburg Press and Amy Cianci, thank you for being my "publishing doula" and reminding me to breathe through the birthing process of this book.

And to you, the reader, thank you for holding space for this book, whether you are reading for yourself, for someone you love, or simply to better understand experiences that are often difficult to name.

What is written here continues beyond these pages, in the ways we notice, remember, and stay.

When you are finished reading, you may choose to pause, to reflect, to share this book with someone, or to return to it another day. There is no right way to carry what you've encountered here. There is only the permission to move forward in a way that feels steady and kind to you.

ABOUT THE AUTHOR

Julie A. Rocco is an internationally emerging voice in suicide prevention, mental health advocacy, and trauma-informed storytelling. As both a suicide loss survivor and a suicide ideation and attempt survivor, her lived experience catalyzed a commitment to challenging silence and expanding how we talk about suicide and mental health in public spaces.

She is the founder of What I Would Have Missed, a movement dedicated to preventing suicide and promoting mental wellness by cultivating connection, camaraderie, and community. Through writing, speaking, art, and community gatherings, Julie works to shift the narrative from isolation to connection and from individual blame to collective responsibility. She believes suicide prevention and mental wellness require both personal courage and systemic awareness, recognizing that access to care, community support, and cultural conditions shape who receives care and who is left to struggle alone.

Her work seeks to elevate and amplify the authentic voices of suicide ideation, attempt, and loss survivors across multiple platforms, including an international podcast, social media, theatre, and the more recent development of a YouTube docuseries blending lived experience with data to deepen public understanding. As a trained facilitator with with certifications in Mental Health First Aide, brain health and integrative behavioral health, and a background in systems change, collaboration, community power-building, and community development, Julie bridges professional expertise with lived truth, meeting people where they are while advocating for broader cultural and structural change as well as redistribution of narrative power.

Julie's work stands on a simple but urgent belief: when we allow stories to be shared in their full expression by those who have lived them, we create the conditions for courage and connection. And, connection saves lives.